'A Sea of Talk'

edited by

John Dwyer

Primary English Teaching Association
NSW, Australia

Heinemann
Portsmouth, New Hampshire

Heinemann Educational Books, Inc.
361 Hanover Street   Portsmouth, NH 03801
Offices and agents throughout the world

Copyright©Primary English Teaching Association, 1989.
PO Box 167   Rozelle NSW 2039   Australia

First U.S. printing 1991

Library of Congress Cataloging-in-Publication Data
"A Sea of talk" / edited by John Dwyer
     p.   cm.
     Includes bibliographical references (p.   )
     ISBN 0-435-08582-4
     1. Oral communication – Study and teaching (Elementary)
  2. Listening.   3. Language arts (Elementary)   I. Dwyer, John.
  LB1572.S43   1989
  372.6 -- dc20   90-27279
                                                                         CIP

Cover design by Wladislaw Finne
Edited and designed by Jeremy V. Steele
Design consultant: Mark Jackson
Typeset in 12/13 Baskerville by Tensor Pty Ltd
40-44 Red Lion Street Rozelle NSW 2039

Printed in the United States of America
91 92 93 94 95   9 8 7 6 5 4 3 2 1

Foreword

How tentative we were in the early seventies as we debated the place of talk — speaking, we called it — in the English language arts curriculum. We all knew it had a place, but there seemed to be many reasons why we couldn't give it due regard. After all, children had plenty of opportunities to talk outside the classroom; talk in the classroom took quite a deal of time and energy to organise; and besides, parents expected learning to read and write to be given pre-eminence in what was already becoming an overcrowded curriculum!

We engaged in numerous conversations and discussions among ourselves and with overseas colleagues, such as Paula Menyuk and Roger Shuy from the United States, and James Britton, Connie and Harold Rosen, Douglas Barnes, Michael Halliday and Joan Tough from the United Kingdom. As we talked we came to understand that talk in the curriculum was important not only in its own right but also because it underpinned each child's 'breakthrough to literacy'.

We came to understand that for children, as well as for ourselves, talk was a very important means of expressing and communicating ideas, thoughts and feelings, and that there were different kinds of talk, different according to who you were, to whom you were talking and the situations in which you found yourself. Above all, we came to understand that talk not only had an important place in the English language arts curriculum but also across the whole curriculum.

Before too long, we came to understand that our (professional) interest in talk was matched only by children's natural curiosity about their own talk and the talk of others. 'Talking about talk' began to emerge as a new, exciting area for our work in curriculum development.

We were convinced, but what would be the response of children, parents and teachers? What would happen in the classrooms of our schools? Would the 'intentions' of our curriculum guidelines match the 'realities' of practice?

This book seeks to answer these questions and more. In its pages we will find children and teachers who talk with one another, talk about what they are doing 'here and now' in the classroom, and about what they know and feel about events shaping the world beyond the classroom. Sometimes too, we will find they talk with one another about what they think about talk itself. Indeed, a sea of talk!

J.E. Tunstall
Director, Division of Curriculum Services
Queensland Department of Education

Acknowledgements

It is impossible to identify by name the many people — teachers, academics, researchers and writers — whose ideas have contributed to this book. Let me just say a general thankyou to all those people with whom I have discussed language in general, and talk in particular, during the last twenty years.

I must, however, pay special thanks to the members of the Queensland Education Department, Van Leer Foundation Project team who, in the late 1960s and early 1970s, produced a language development program for Aboriginal children in Years 1, 2 and 3. In particular, I want to acknowledge the work of Julia Koppe, who was responsible for the general theoretical direction of that program as well as for many of its day-to-day practical activities. As I look back, it is obvious that Julia was far ahead of her time. It was through her that I became aware of my need to know more about language development and the relationship of language to learning and to self-esteem.

I would also like to acknowledge the support I have received over the years from John Carr, both in his role as a language arts curriculum officer in the Queensland Education Department and as project officer for *Study Talk*, Queensland's contribution to the national CDC Language Development Project in the early 1980s.

My special thanks go, of course, to Jim Tunstall, who wrote the Foreword, and to the teachers who contributed to this book. I very much appreciate the fact that they made time in their busy programs to share the exciting work that they are doing.

I would like to thank Jeremy Steele for his friendly advice and, in particular, for being prepared to work within my time frame. There must have been times when he wondered if he would ever bring this book to press.

I am also grateful to Travis Teske for making available the two photographs which appear in Betty Murray's chapter.

Finally, my thanks go to Lisa Brandt and Cheryl Proellocks who typed (and re-typed) all the drafts of the material in this book.

J.D.

Contents

The Contributors

Jan D'Arcy is Principal of Dagun State School near Gympie, Queensland. At the time of writing she was Principal of the one-teacher Homebush State School. She uses children's literature as a major focus for her classroom programs.

Naida Dwyer is a remedial teacher/consultant in Brisbane, working in the PATCH program (Parents as Tutors of Children). She has taught in many different situations and uses poetry to capture special moments with children.

Margaret Hetherington teaches a Year 1-2 class at Kelso State School in Townsville. She wrote her chapter while teaching Year 1 children at nearby Belgian Gardens State School. She has trialled language arts activities for curriculum officers in the Queensland Education Department.

Betty Murray is an Inspector of Schools in the West Moreton Region of the Queensland Education Department. She was the foundation writer of the Torres Strait English Program and was subsequently appointed as first supervisor of the Far Northern Schools Development Unit (FNSDU) on Thursday Island. She is a former Churchill Fellow and recently spent a year in Scotland undertaking a Master's Degree in Applied Linguistics.

Joy Schloss is a primary-trained teacher who has worked in mainstream classes with high numbers of migrant students. For the last eight years she has worked as an ESL teacher with Immigrant Education, Queensland. She is presently a member of the Language in Learning Project team within Immigrant Education Support Services.

Steve Stronach based his chapter on his work as a classroom teacher at Belgian Gardens State School in Townsville. He and Margaret Hetherington collaborated as 'action researchers', trialling activities for curriculum writers in the Queensland Education Department. He is now working with children who need help with behaviour adjustment and management.

Dian Van Dijk currently teaches Year Five at Strathpine West State School, just north of Brisbane. She has worked on a specially funded program to develop the language of gifted and talented children. For many years she was a language arts adviser.

'He Wants to Write'

Teacher, I wanta write.

Good! That's good! Get some paper.

Teacher, I wanta write now.

O.K. Good! You need paper.

Teacher, what can I write?

Well! Let's think
what you know
what you like
where you go
a story you read
you've got a new bed

But Teacher! You said I could write.

Well! Then do it.

But Teacher! You said we could write
any time we liked.

Yes. I did. And you can.

Well Teacher! Tell me some words.
I need words.
I don't know words
to say what you want.
I wanta write
what you'll like.

Naida Dwyer

'Talking in Class'

John Dwyer

He wants to write. But to write he needs words — words to help him express his ideas and please his audience. To find the words and frame the ideas, he *has* to talk.

> *Reading and writing float on a sea of talk.*
> (Britton 1983)

Children set sail on this 'sea' from a variety of starting points. While some have better navigational aids and more supportive pilots than others, all must plot their own course. Along the way they meet many shoals and often capsize. As they struggle to right themselves, they progressively construct their own chart of the sea — a chart which, over time, more and more closely matches the general chart used by the people in their world.

Sailing from familiar shores, they strike out to discover new worlds in their own heads. Sharing voyages with others, they sail previously uncharted waters to visit unknown lands, exploring them together to uncover their secrets and their wonder.

From time to time they become aware of the sea itself — its features and the conventions required to navigate it successfully.

This book charts parts of this sea and some of these journeys. It looks at children 'setting sail', *learning to talk* in various situations. It describes children exploring new routes and new ideas, *learning through talk*. It eavesdrops on children becoming aware of the sea itself, *learning about talk*. It focusses also on the talk of teachers as they help children navigate their journey.

In short, this book is about talk — the talk of children and teachers in classrooms.

> *Language is the naming of experience, and what we name we have power over.*
> (Kingman 1988, p. 7)

Talking is our prime means of communication. We talk in response to events and in preparation for action. We talk to define ourselves *to ourselves* and to others. We talk to define the situation and our place in it. We talk to establish, strengthen or end personal relationships. We receive and develop ideas and explore our understandings initially through talk.

Through talk we persuade, explain, instruct, entertain, narrate, speculate, argue a case, report, describe, find out, express feelings, clarify or explore an issue, solve a problem, interpret, summarise, evaluate, reflect, announce, criticise and deal with criticism.

Children, too, need to use talk for all these purposes. Are our classrooms talking places? Are they places which encourage tentative and exploratory talk; which allow children to talk through their problems, discuss their tasks, clarify their thoughts, and express their joys and fears? Are they places where children are given opportunities to reflect upon differences in language which are determined by different contexts, audiences and purposes?

Are they, in fact, places where children learn to talk; learn through talk; and learn about talk?

The value of talk in all curriculum areas as a means of promoting pupils' understanding and of evaluating their progress is now widely accepted. During the past twenty-five years the contribution of talk has been endorsed in all major educational reports in the United States, the United Kingdom and Australia. It has been supported by Mathematics and Science Teachers' Associations as well as by Associations for the Teaching of English and by the UK Association for Primary Education.

One of the most recent reports, *National Curriculum: English for Ages 5-11,* released in the United Kingdom in November 1988, provides a good summary of current attitudes to and beliefs about talking and listening. Asserting that interactive spoken language is widely recognised as a powerful means of learning, it proposes that children should be able to understand the spoken word and express themselves effectively in a variety of speaking and listening activities, matching style and response to audience and purpose (p. 35).

To achieve these goals children should encounter an extensive range of materials, situations and activities, planned to develop their capacity and confidence in talking and listening. These situations should allow for talking and listening with peers and adults across curriculum areas and in a wide range of groupings — pairs, small groups, whole class groups, and groups larger than the class. Children should be encouraged to develop speaking and listening skills both 'in-role' (as themselves) and 'out-of-role' (through role play and drama).

Teaching should develop, by informal means and in the course of purposeful activities, children's powers of attention and grasp of turn-taking. Such teaching should help children gain and hold the attention of listeners.

Children should also be helped to learn how to disagree courteously with an opposing point of view.

Talking activities should develop children's grasp of sequence, cause and effect, reasoning, sense of consistency, appreciation of relevance and irrelevance, and powers of prediction and recall.

Through all of these activities children should be helped, mostly informally and indirectly, to extend and adjust their ways of speaking and listening according to purpose and context (see p. 37).

If children are going to achieve these goals, teachers need to organise learning and teaching in ways which build logically and consistently on the successful language learning that children have already accomplished in their own homes and communities.

David Allen, writing in 1988 on behalf of the UK National Association of Advisers in English, spelt this out in terms of learner and teacher needs as follows:

> ... *the learner needs*
>
> > *expectation of success,*
> >
> > *the confidence to take risks and make mistakes,*
> >
> > *a willingness to share and engage,*
> >
> > *the confidence to ask for help,*
> >
> > *an acceptance of the need to readjust,*
>
> *and the teacher needs*
>
> > *respect for and interest in the learner's language culture, thought and intentions,*
> >
> > *the ability to recognise growth points, strengths and potential,*
> >
> > *the appreciation that mistakes are necessary to learning,*
> >
> > *the confidence to maintain breadth, richness and variety, and to match these to the learner's interests and direction (i.e. to stimulate and challenge),*
> >
> > *a sensitive awareness of when to intervene and when to leave alone.*
>
> (cited in *English for Ages 5-11,* p. 7)

Sadly, there is often a gap between ideal curricula in oral language as proposed by educationists and actual curricula and practice in schools. This became very clear to me in the early 1980s when I chaired the management committee of *Study Talk,* a Curriculum Development Centre (CDC) Language Development Project sponsored by education authorities in Queensland.

One of the important objectives of the *Study Talk* project was to investigate what people directly and indirectly involved in schools thought about talk and about its place in upper primary and lower secondary schooling. Their responses, published in Carr 1984, generated a number of conclusions.

Many people found it difficult to talk about talk. They had little explicit knowledge about language. They used a fairly limited range of terms and discussed relatively few concepts. On the other hand, they'd learned to operate effectively without such explicit knowledge. In fact, on the basis of limited information, some had developed very firmly held views about language and were often quite censorious of people who violated these 'folk-linguistic' beliefs.

Many people seemed to have little awareness of the role language played in their life. They were often unaware of the ways they used language themselves or of the ways it was used on or against them. They seemed to have little understanding of the way that children's language develops or of the ways in which language varies within the one speaker, from person to person, from time to time, and within and between speech and writing.

Views expressed on the role of talk in the curriculum were relatively unsophisticated. There was little awareness of the potential value of talk in school. On the other hand there was a clear recognition of difficulties encountered in planning and managing activities involving student talk. Clearly, many teachers saw such activities as threatening.

Inadequacies in children's language were largely seen in terms of vocabulary and lack of self-confidence. Few teachers, parents or children could think of a wide range of language activities. There was support for the value of talk for learning in the 'content' areas but there were considerable restrictions placed upon it. It would seem that many people held a 'transmission' model of learning/teaching. Few people seemed to be aware that children and adults might better grasp new understandings by talking about them.

Before too much is made of these conclusions, it is important to acknowledge a number of points.

- The sample of people interviewed was relatively small.

- The focus was on upper primary and lower secondary schooling. The balance of responses might have been different if the survey had sought opinions across the total primary school spectrum.

- The survey was conducted in 1981 and reported in 1984. Knowledge and attitudes may have changed in the intervening years.

You might like to test the last two possibilities. It could be interesting and valuable (and fun) to try out all or some of the five survey questions on adults and children around you so that you can make your own judgements.

- Do you think that children should talk in the classroom?

- Do you think that talking about a subject will help children understand it better?

- What kinds of language do you think children should use when they talk in class?

- Do you think that children's ability to talk effectively can be developed by planned oral language lessons in school?

- Do you think that children should be taught about language in school?

You might like to check the responses you get against those given below, which represent what the writers of this book would say.

Do you think that children should talk in the classroom?

The answer to this question has to be a resounding 'Yes'.

Through talk children negotiate not only their own learning but also their place in the classroom world and beyond. Accordingly *all* children must be given opportunities to develop the ability to talk in a variety of settings, for their own benefit and for the general good of our society.

> *A democratic society needs people who have the linguistic abilities which will enable them to discuss, evaluate and make sense of what they are told, as well as to take effective action on the basis of their understanding.... Otherwise there can be no genuine participation but only the imposition of the ideas of those who are linguistically capable.*
>
> (Kingman 1988, p. 7)

Do you think that talking about a subject will help children understand it better?

Again the answer has to be an emphatic 'Yes'.

Talk is central to learning. Through talk we clarify our own understandings. Through talk we negotiate the construction of shared meanings (Wells 1977).

It is a theme which recurs frequently throughout this book. We hear how talking supports reading and writing. We observe dialect-speaking and non-English-speaking children using talk as a bridge from their own language to the language and learning demands of the English-speaking school. We note in passing brief snippets of talk as children develop understandings in a range of subject areas.

What kinds of language do you think children should use in class?

Many of the respondents to the original survey saw the classroom as a fairly formal place where only 'good English' was appropriate. While some teachers recognised the need for informal language to be used in school, many seemed to equate informal language with slang or 'swearing'. Some respondents were angry when non-English (or dialect) speakers used their first language in school.

Many of these responses derived from a concern for 'correctness', although respondents often had difficulty in defining that term and in identifying the authority by which 'correctness' was established.

While this book acknowledges the existence, and importance, of defined standards in areas of language performance, it is particularly concerned with the concept of 'appropriateness' — with the use and acceptance of talk which is appropriate to the needs of the context within which the talk is occurring.

A persistent theme is the critical relationship between the child's success in talking and listening and the respect accorded to the child and to his or her attempts at talking and listening.

This relationship holds true for all children, but it is even more significant for the child who brings to the school a non-English language or a non-Standard dialect of English.

> ... *language above all else is the defining characteristic of an individual, a community, a nation.*
>
> (Kingman 1988, p. 43)

> *Pupils will be assisted in developing a language repertoire ... by teachers who recognise the intimate links between dialect and identity ...; who understand the damage to self-esteem and motivation done by indiscriminate 'correction' of dialect forms ...; and who are, nevertheless, capable of being explicit, when necessary, about the character and place of Standard English and its forms ....*
>
> (English for Ages 5-11, p. 35)

Each child's talk provides a base on which further language development can be built. This 'building' is strengthened when the teacher resists the temptation to make assumptions about the child's language ability on the basis of limited or inappropriate data. Accordingly a related theme running through the book is the need to assess children's talk in ways which neither disadvantage children nor distort or limit productive teaching and learning activities.

Do you think that children's ability to talk effectively can be developed by planned oral language lessons in school?

Clearly, the teachers who have described their work in this book have shown that the answer to this question must be 'Yes'.

These teachers explain how purposeful contexts for talk can be developed in the classroom. But they also remind us that the children in any class group will display a wide range of language abilities, and so a wide range of experiences and a variety of teaching and learning contexts must be provided. Equally, they stress the importance of classroom organisation and negotiated rules and routines in fostering the development of talk for learning.

They also highlight the need for direct teacher modelling if children are to master the conventions and demands of talk in different contexts. While their major focus remains always on meaning, they point out the need to provide children with some structure if they are to master various genres, or if they are to become aware of differences between standard forms and usages and their own non-standard performance.

> *... pupils need to have their attention drawn to what they are doing and why they are doing it ....*

(Kingman 1988, p. 13)

Do you think that children should be taught about *language in school*? Again the answer is 'Yes'.

Children need a language to help them talk about language. They need to know, and be able to talk about, the conventions of various genres.

Some of the writers in this book have emphasised the need for teachers, too, to know more about language development, language structure and language terminology.

Teachers probably need to become more aware of the significance of their own talk within the classroom. They are are often surprised when they realise the extent to which they dominate the talk which occurs in their classrooms and the frequency with which they break the established 'rules' for classroom interaction.

Teachers may also need to reflect on how their attitudes towards individual children, and their expectations of them, are transmitted through their talk.

This book focusses on talking and listening, aspects of language which have been somewhat neglected in recent literature.

It describes children and teachers learning to talk in various ways to achieve various purposes. It shows children learning through talk. It urges all of us to learn more about talk—both the talk used by the children in our classrooms and the teacher talk that we use in them.

I hope that it will convince you that talk is worth talking about and listening to. It will be successful to the extent that it challenges you to think about, and perhaps modify, your attitudes and practices concerning *talking in class.*

'Talking and Listening in Year One'

Margaret Hetherington

In my Year One classroom I encourage my twenty children to talk, listen, observe, enjoy, explore, examine and share. My child-centred program tries to provide genuine purposes for listening, talking, reading and writing.

I'd like to share some of the ideas and practices I've developed and used successfully. Although these were developed for my Year One class, I'm sure they can be adapted for older children.

Listening

The listener must take an active part in listening.

> *Listening is a combination of hearing what another person says and a suspenseful waiting, an intense psychological involvement with a person talking.*
> (Bolton 1987, p. 32)

Children are sometimes encouraged to be passive recipients of information, with the result that they may learn not to listen at all.

'We don't listen to those things.'

'Don't pay any attention to him.'

'Ignore it.'

Although they are immersed in sound all day, children rarely have good listening demonstrated.

> *...active listening carries two risks: the exposure of the way we really are and the possibility of becoming different.... effective interpersonal communication requires both inner security and personal courage.*
> (Gordon 1976, p. 83)

I believe that self-esteem is essential for successful listening.

'Am I really prepared to listen to what people say to me?'
'Am I prepared to be changed by what I hear?'

Strategies to develop active listening

1 Use body language, e.g:

- leaning forward
- looking at the speaker
- allowing the face to show feeling: surprise, interest, disbelief.

2 Talk about body language.

'People communicate with their bodies.'
'When you look at me it tells me that you're interested in what I'm saying.'
'When your eyes are wide open it tells me you're alert.' (I missed a fact on TV the other day. Jasmine said, 'You couldn't have been alert, Mrs H.')

3 Speak quietly.

4 Only say things once. (Establish this rule at the beginning of the year.)

5 Talk about listening.

'Why is listening important?'
'How do you know people are listening to you?'
'Do you believe that what you have to say is important?'

Use a classroom meeting to discuss these and other ideas.

6 Try not to repeat what a child has said. In my experience, if children know you are going to say it again, they think there's no need for them to listen the first time. The speaker also says to him/herself, 'There's no need to speak up.'
   Ask other children if they agree/disagree: 'What do you think about that?'

7 Encourage more than one child to answer the same question.

8 Use signals other than the voice to change activities — music, hand signs, or walking over to groups — instead of making grand announce-ments all the time.

9 Pause often when speaking. Not every waking moment needs to be filled with the sound of your voice.

10 Allow children time to answer questions. Give everyone's wheels time to move.

11 Model listening!

12 Provide for lots of talking time, e.g. after assemblies, or in classroom meetings.

Give children the opportunity to show that they were listening

1 Ask the children to tell the person beside them what was just said.

2 Ask the children to close their eyes and make a list of the important information in their heads. Then ask them to turn to a partner and work out the facts together.

Listening partners

3 In group work ask one child to report the group's findings.

4 Before a TV program give the children something to listen for, e.g:
'Listen for the part of the program that tells you how the young monkeys learn about their place in the group through their games.'

5 After a TV program ask the children to turn to a friend and tell what they learned or what they found interesting.

Keep a record of the development of listening and speaking skills

1 Walk around and sit in on groups or pairs; join in and listen.

2 Keep anecdotal records. (The children have become used to me and my scribble book!)

3 Use tape recordings.

4 The children can also keep self-evaluation records. Brendan's, shown opposite, may be transcribed thus:

> *I learnt how to sit up straight.*
> *I learnt how to listen and look at the person's eyes while they're speaking.*
> *I learnt how to sing.*
> *I learnt how to be silent while eating.*
> *I learnt how to be sensible while interviewing.*
> *1988 is important because there is a lot of things happening all the time.*

Teacher evaluation

I acquired the checklist shown overleaf at a seminar conducted by Libby Knight, who had adapted it from Montgomery (1982). I found it covered the questions I had been asking myself.

Talking

Strategies to develop children's talk

1 Ensure that talk is purposeful and arises out of meaningful learning tasks.

2 Model the language the children need.

3 Allow lots of time for talk. We talk most of the day. Out of an hour's writing session we write for twenty minutes.

4 Use children as interaction models, e.g: 'Please look at how Kelly and Jasmine are having a Partner Conference.'

5 Set the routines at the beginning of the year and build on them. They are integral to the success of the program. The routines are more important at first. The quality of interaction then develops its own momentum.

SELF-EVALUATION CHECKLIST

	Yes	No	Needs Reflection
Am I defeating good listening by talking too much?			
Do I realise that children have difficulty listening attentively for a long period of time?			
Do I vary my style of presentation in order to encourage children to listen?			
Do I expect children to concentrate on too many things at a time?			
Do I give children time to find the answer to one question before another is asked?			
Do I ask open-ended questions that do not require right or wrong answers? Are my explanations clearly presented?			
Do I try not to repeat what each child says, but rather require the class to concentrate on the child speaking?			
Am I taking too much time in explaining to one child while others lose interest?			
Do I try not to repeat phrases or expressions so often that they become ineffective and monotonous?			
Do I treat the children's opinions with respect?			
Am I getting the full attention of the class before giving information?			
Do I make myself available for listening? Do children feel free to come to me with their problems and know they will have my undivided attention?			

Over the next week I will try to build my skills in the following areas.

After trying this I observed that...

Some purposeful contexts for talk

The Guest Writer

SETTING
One child, the guest writer, is seated in the writer's chair with the other children and the teacher on the mat. The activity lasts for about 5 to 10 minutes and usually takes place at the end of a writing session.

OBJECTIVES
- To give the writer an opportunity to present work and receive immediate feedback.
- To provide a model of a particular aspect of writing, e.g. a successful report or recount, or an example of effective word usage.
- To model for children, and have them use, appropriate 'responding' language.

PROCEDURE
Introduction — I give a spoken 'blurb' about the author (the guest writer) and draw attention to the point I want to highlight.

Reading — At the beginning of the year children volunteered to read their pieces of writing. I encouraged this to develop confidence. By the end of the year I was asking the guest writer not only to read but to focus on a particular aspect of the writing, e.g. the plot, or the use of adverbs. Sometimes the guest writer is selected to allow us all to celebrate the writer's growth.

Response — From the beginning it was established as a rule that the first response must start with 'I like...' . The task is to help fellow writers develop by talking about what is successful. For instance, when Bryony read her story, Kirsty said, 'I like how you did the shivering words and the thunderstorm at the end.'

Interviewing — This is not a show and tell session in which the audience are passive onlookers, and the interview segment demands active listening. It was introduced after many how and why questions had been modelled and discussed. So, after the positive response to Bryony's story, Natalie was able to ask, 'How come you did it that way?' and Carolyn followed with, 'Are you pleased with your work?'

OUTCOMES

The children learn a tremendous amount from each other about audience, structure, sequence and using effective words at these sessions. The emphasis is on developing self-confidence as a writer and, later, on the ability to receive constructive criticism.

The children respond enthusiastically to the guest writer, who reads with the expectation that it will be a positive, helpful experience.

Writers' Circle

SETTING

This activity takes 10-15 minutes and occurs every day. A group of five children sit with me in a circle on a mat. The other children are doing quiet work at the tables. The routine is built up gradually over time. About 2-3 minutes are spent on each child's writing. Although the process is similar to that of 'Guest Writer', the group is smaller and more informal and the children are reacting to each other's draft writing.

OBJECTIVES

- To conference writers.
- To model appropriate language.
- To develop critical thinking skills.
- To intervene on a teaching point.
- To record each child's development.
- To learn about what the child knows.
- To share.

PROCEDURE

Introduction/Orientation — I remind the children of the rules that we have established over time.

> 'This is a Writer's Circle. You've each brought a piece of your writing to share. You may have a problem you need help with, or you may wish to read a part you're pleased with. You all take turns and it's each writer's responsibility to listen to and encourage other writers.'

Reading/Response — This process is repeated for each writer. As an illustration, here's some of the discussion which followed Warren's reading of his letter to Susie.

NATALIE: Do you want this to really show Susie that you're trying your best?

WARREN: I might put...

NATALIE: No. That wasn't my question. Do you really want to *show* this to Susie?

WARREN: Yes.

NATALIE: Well I think you need to work on that bit.
(We had been talking about using words to show and not just tell.)

BAYANI: I just like all those words, Warren.

TEACHER: I like the way you have your plans worked out.

KIRSTY: I like how you did 'love from' and I know how to spell 'love'.

TAMARA: I like how you thought about her name. I like how you spelt birthday. What's this black thing?

OUTCOMES

As the year goes by I find that the children use the language I have modelled. They listen to each other and they grow as writers because of this interaction. They develop critical thinking skills. I am able to sit back more often and just take my notes. I particularly like to look for the degree of confidence exhibited by each child, and for each child's ability to express him/herself. I also learn a lot more about what the children know.

Partner Conferences

SETTING

I use Partner Conferences throughout the day. Some take place before writing and some afterwards.

Because I like children to be on task and to be working quietly when they are at their tables, I conference with them on the mat. Similarly, partner conferences take place on the mat.

OBJECTIVES

- To develop the skills of listening, questioning and discussion.
- To encourage children to reflect on and evaluate their work.

PROCEDURE

Planning — Planning with partners helps children establish what they know, how they know it, and how they are going to show that they know it.

For children thinking about a piece they have not yet begun to write, the steps run like this.

1 Close your eyes, and bring your piece of writing to mind.
2 Think what your plans are for today.
3 Tell your partner.

> NATALIE: I'm going to write about when I burnt my arm. There's
> · a lesson in my story too.

For children already engaged in writing, the routine is varied.

1 Bring the piece of writing you are working on to the mat.
2 Re-read it.
3 Ask yourself what your plans are?
4 Tell the person beside you.

> LEIGH: What are your plans, Kirsty?
> KIRSTY: I'm writing about Willows Water World.
> LEIGH: I'm writing about the ghost. They climb up the stairs and
> they look through the door... when they open up the door
> there is a witch in there ....

Reflecting — The children share the work completed for the day. They ask themselves, 'What have I got done?' and tell their partner about it.

Partners use language modelled at Writers' Circle. Sometimes I prompt a fresh direction for their discussion.

> 'Ask your partner a "how" question.'
>
> 'Tell your partner what you are pleased with.'

I often ask children to demonstrate

- looking at a person
- showing interest
- a terrific question.

The Class Meeting

SETTING

Class meetings are held regularly on Mondays and Wednesdays, but they are also called whenever I feel it's necessary to sit down and say, 'Hey, let's look at this problem!' The meetings are only 15 minutes long. We all sit on the mat. It's important to have a circle with no gaps to create the feeling of belonging.

OBJECTIVES
- To solve problems.
- To reflect.
- To philosophise.
- To develop trust.
- To encourage assertiveness.
- To develop self-esteem.
- To encourage children to make self-referent ('I') statements.

PROCEDURE

Introduction — I usually re-state the rules of discourse each time.

> 'This is a meeting to which people can bring their problems. We take turns to speak. And we listen to what other people have to say.'

Discussion — The children are encouraged to make 'I' statements.

> 'I am happy about....'
>
> 'I am sad about....'

We discuss trust, rules, and the importance of individuals and groups. I find that sometimes I expand the children's statements.

> 'Those are good examples to show that you like the way they co-operated.'

> 'Yes, you've really shown us we can trust people.'

I often ask children to clarify statements or to predict outcomes.

Not all children speak to the whole group. As Timothy told me, 'I don't have to say it if I think someone else has said it.' However, all the children have the opportunity to speak to a partner later in order to express their ideas.

OUTCOMES

We really enjoy these meetings. The format and routines were introduced early in the year and we have extended them gradually as the year has progressed. At first I did most of the talking, but now the children talk freely and use the meetings to solve problems.

I was delighted recently when Natalie said to me, 'Mrs H, we'll need to have a meeting to talk about....'

Conclusion

Observing and documenting the range of talk used by my Year One children has been exciting and rewarding. I have learnt a lot more about myself and my teaching. I have confirmed my belief that a child's success in speaking and listening is directly related to the respect accorded to that child. But above all I have learnt a great deal about the children. I am constantly surprised and delighted by what they know and what they can talk about. They are well on their way to being 'action researchers' — people who submit their practice to critical self-appraisal.

'Talking in the Reading Conference'

Jan D'Arcy

Reading conferences have been introduced as a key element in the development of a 'whole language approach' across my school — a one-teacher school with twenty-two children, representing all year levels. My own belief is that a holistic approach to language learning is best supported and extended by the use of real books (both fiction and non-fiction) to foster language development. My ultimate aim has been to create a rich literature environment based on an integrated listening/speaking/reading/writing model.

Books need to be shared by a community of readers. Encouraging children to discuss their responses with their peers and their teacher generates and extends ideas and understandings. It's also a very effective way of getting children to share their enthusiasms and recommend books to each other.

Over the course of a year, reading conferences have become a critical component of my language program. I have found they provide:

- a forum for children's discussion
- an opportunity for me to model ways of responding orally to literature, and
- an informal means for the sharing of enjoyable, sometimes memorable experiences.

They also enable me to monitor children's reading interests and progress, and to help those who are having difficulty in selecting appropriate books.

A literature-based language program

I use literature, both fiction and non-fiction, as the springboard for many activities. I find that reading books to the children, sometimes in serial-

ised form, provides almost limitless opportunities for the sharing and enjoyment of literature and for the modelling of oral and written responses to
literature. For this daily reading I try to choose books which capture the
children's interest, which relate to a current theme, which illustrate specific
features, and which generate a range of responses.

My key program components are:

- daily silent reading of self-selected materials
- daily teacher reading to the children
- language contracts focussing on a theme
- reading activities related to class and individual books
- daily writing, usually related to the contract/theme
- oral sharing sessions of reading and writing activities.

I introduced reading conferences to link various elements of this literature-
based language program together.

In the reading conferences we cooperatively explore examples of plot
structure, characterisation, author style, theme and genre. Using group
talk we prepare for, and model, a range of language activities — plot pro-
files, story maps, comparisons and contrasts, literary interviews, literary
report cards, diaries and letters to the author.

For example, as part of our 'Adventure Theme', I read Colin Thiele's
Coorong Captive to the children. Our conferences about this book covered
a range of activities designed to broaden children's understanding of story
elements and how these elements work together to make the story enjoyable and interesting.

As a class we brainstormed a list of the most important plot events, in
time sequence. This involved a lot of discussion because we wanted a
summary of only the most significant incidents. Each incident was then
rated for excitement, and plotted on a simple line graph. Our resulting
plot profile increased children's awareness of how Colin Thiele had built
up the action to a climax, and then very effectively completed his story.
(I also found that further group and individual work of this kind fostered
the children's personal narrative writing, which began to show their greater
awareness of how stories develop.)

We kept a large version of our plot profile on display in the classroom,
using it as a focal reference point for further activities. The class was broken
into four groups and each group was allocated a section of the plot from
which to develop a literary interview. The groups devised lists of interview
questions for a television reporter covering Fitzie's heroic adventure and
drafted Fitzie's responses. Two group members then role-played their
group's interview and the rest of the class helped edit and revise so that
a final, complete interview could be written. Later each interview was performed before a parent audience.

Equally successful was the creation of a *Coorong Captive* game, which used the characters, setting and plot events. All children contributed ideas to a master plan from which a game with question and answer cards, directions and penalties/rewards was refined. The game was constructed and illustrated by the children, and proved to be both a worthwhile learning activity and a popular rainy day pastime.

Other activities, including a character comparison between Fitzie and Goondalee and letters to the author, complemented and extended our discussions of *Coorong Captive*.

Group discussions like these, supplemented by individual reading conferences with me, have allowed the children to draw upon in-depth, wide-ranging experiences in making rudimentary generalisations about themes, characterisation, plot structures and styles of writing. At the same time their appreciation and enjoyment of literature have been heightened and their personal responses fostered by the exchange of ideas in a supportive environment.

Developing the reading conference

During the year three types of reading conference evolved. We began with four interest-based groups. Members reported to the group on the book they were currently reading or had recently finished reading.

Because the children had some difficulty with the openness of this approach, we moved into more focussed group conferences where discussion was based on authors, themes, or a particular book.

Later individual conferences were also introduced. Usually these formed part of a language contract which required the child to discuss one or more books with me.

Talking in these various kinds of reading conference helped children to:

- explore ideas about plot development, characterisation, theme, style and use of language
- seek information
- discuss with other readers what a text (or part of it) might mean
- reflect on language use, and the special effects an author can create through choice of language
- share feelings — of enjoyment, sadness, hope, frustration
- exchange recommendations for future reading
- appreciate the point of view of others.

To help children prepare themselves, we established some pre-conference requirements.

WHAT TO BRING TO A READING CONFERENCE!

Always bring   ● the book to be discussed

                      ● your written reading log comment.

You may bring   ● a written comment on style/theme/
                        characterisation

                      ● a picture of the main character or setting

                      ● a list of important characters with brief
                        descriptions

                      ● a marked part of the book to share

                      ● a list of major events and settings.

Despite this preparation, some children still felt daunted by the prospect of talking about books with their peers. They lacked experience in organising their ideas, expressing opinions and listening to others, and so were unable to give thoughtful feedback. It became evident very early on that help was necessary.

I used three main strategies to help children organise their thoughts for oral sharing.

(1) Teacher modelling

The first strategy involved my modelling questions and responses which showed that I was interested in what the speaker had to say and that I had listened. These are the kinds of issues that I raised.

Characterisation

● Who are the main characters in the story? Which character do you like best? Why?

● Can you identify with any of the characters in this book? In what ways?

● Is there a character in the book you'd like as a friend? What character traits appeal to you?

● Is there a character you don't like? What sort of person is he/she?

Plot

● Can you briefly retell the main events in the story?

● Do you think the ending is effective? If you were the author, would you change it? How?

- Which part of the story do you find most exciting/interesting/memorable/amusing?

- What is the climax of the story? How is the problem/dilemma resolved?

Setting

- Where and when does the story take place?

- Does the setting play an important part in the story?

General

- What's your opinion of this book? Would you recommend it to any classmates?

- Have you read any other books by this author? Do you intend to now?

- How would you describe the author's style?

- Was the story intended to be true to life? What do you think is the author's message?

Before long I found that the children also began to ask these kinds of questions and discuss these sorts of issues.

(2) Written reading activities

My second strategy was to encourage children to use written reading activities as a stimulus for oral discussion. Here are some examples.

- Write a comment telling why you enjoyed/disliked the book.

- Draw a cartoon strip or a set of illustrations showing the main events in sequence.

- Compare (named) characters in the book/in different books.

- Construct a semantic web for the story.

- Prepare a poster advertising the book.

- Make up a game based on this book or on other book(s) by this author.

- Write a different ending for the book (or a chapter in it).

- Draw a time-line of (character's) life.

- Prepare a wanted/missing person poster for (character).

- Write a letter to (character), or between (characters).

Storm Boy
Colin Thiele

1. What did you think of this book?

2. What did you like best about it? Why?

3. How did you feel about Storm Boy? Why?

4. Did the author describe the setting well? How?

5. What audience do you think Colin Thiele had in mind?

6. Have you read any other books by Colin Thiele?

7. Are there any of his books you would like to read?

8. What message was the author trying to get across?

- Construct a story map or a story ladder.

- Prepare a plot profile.

- Write a newspaper report based on part of the book.

- Compile a literary sociogram.

(See Johnson and Louis 1987 and Hornsby et al. 1986)

(3) Reading conference guide sheets

My third strategy was to encourage children to fill out reading conference guide sheets beforehand, so that they could reflect on pertinent issues and refer to their written responses during the conference. A sample is shown opposite.

I also sought to provide support by encouraging other types of oral response to books. We held panel discussions, prepared TV and radio advertisements, and conducted 'radio interviews' with characters or authors. The children used puppets to retell stories. They prepared and performed plays based on books they'd read or they role-played characters in a book.

All of these conference-related activities helped develop the children's self-confidence as speakers and as readers interacting with authors' ideas.

Developing children's conference abilities

Looking back over my planning diary reminds me that developing this self-confidence took time and effort, as the following passages show.

General Plan

Aim

To promote talking in a rich literature environment in which children read for enjoyment and are willing to discuss their responses to books they have read, thus extending their reading interests and understandings.

Action Steps

- Introduce group reading conferences. Negotiate expectations for conference preparation with children.

- Focus initially on children's own choice of books and personal responses.

- Encourage response through open-ended questions and interaction with others who have read book(s).

- Keep anecdotal records during conferences.

Reflection

- Time! I find that it's time-consuming to record observations and so I can't be involved in discussions, even though it has become obvious that I need to do more modelling of ways of responding to literature.

- Some children and groups are very enthusiastic and well-prepared, but those who aren't tend to launch into complicated, disjointed, boring retellings of plot. We need to keep negotiating what is required for a conference.

Revised General Plan 1

Action Steps

- To overcome lack of variety and depth in children's responses and their presentation, greater emphasis to be placed on written reading activities.

- Introduce group conferences based on a particular book. Children to volunteer for particular conferences, and to complete a reading conference guide sheet designed to provoke thought before they speak to the group.

- Tape some conferences to encourage further discussion and feedback.

Reflection

- Still fairly simple responses. Most children can cope with memory questions but have difficulty in interpreting author intentions and in analysing their own feelings/responses.

- Responses often lack insight. I need to give more help with discussions about feelings/thoughts/ideas.

- Some children are not transferring ideas from written reading activities (usually well done) to oral discussion. Are they scared to voice opinions in front of others or do they just find it difficult to express their ideas in speech?

- Children really enjoy group conferences on a specific book. They still need teacher help but they are far more motivated than when sharing reading activities on a range of books.

- Children enjoy preparing and using a written reading activity, as well as a reading conference guide sheet, to stimulate discussion.

Revised General Plan 2

Action Steps

- Continue group conferences and introduce individual conferences as part of individual language contracts to provide reinforcement of aspects of conferencing according to individual needs.

Reflection

- Interaction between students in group conferences showing improvement. More children are now prepared to offer opinions without my direction, although there is an ongoing need for input from me — modelling of responses, genuine discussion of books, whole class construction of reading activities that focus on specific elements of books, introduction to new authors/genres/styles of writing.

- Greater awareness of authors and books is now evident, as is understanding of elements of plot, character development, setting, etc. in discussion and comments.

- Children are developing a language repertoire for the discussion of books.

- This greater understanding of elements of story structure and language use is reflected in the children's writing, e.g. in developing outlines (plot events, setting, character, genre) before writing.

- Group conferences seem to offer best value-for-time, but individual conferences have a place and are useful in helping children develop as readers and thoughtful responders to literature.

Some conclusions

The success of reading conferences depends upon the children's ability to take responsibility for their own learning. They must have considered the issues to be discussed so that they can speak coherently and really present their own ideas and views. It is essential that children accept the challenge and begin to take the initiative in asking questions of others and justifying their own comments.

I find that children will talk more readily in response to their friends' statements than in response to direct teacher questions. For example:

JASON: How did you feel about Elmer?

WARREN: I feel sorry.

JASON: So do I. Why do you feel sorry?

WARREN: I feel sorry because he's always getting picked on. Like when he was on the wharf and in that laboratory.

Conferences are most useful when children have been 'trained' to express opinions and refer to particular incidents in books rather than giving overall impressions. Our early conferences were very teacher-dominated, but the children gradually accepted more and more responsibility. At first, children who were not well prepared were usually unable to progress beyond jumbled plot retellings. There was definite improvement with the introduction of closer links between written reading activities and conferences on particular books, themes or authors.

Reading conferences stimulated a greater awareness of authors and books. Children developed an oral language repertoire for the discussion of books. They referred comfortably to 'theme', 'plot', 'characterisation', 'setting', and elements of each. These understandings were reflected in their pre-writing, writing and writing conference behaviours.

While the emphasis in reading conferences was always on sharing rather than testing, these conferences did provide me with an invaluable source of data for anecdotal evaluative records on aspects of a child's total language development. I regularly made brief notes about each child's oral responses in reading conferences, using sheets like the one shown opposite.

A final word

I believe that reading conferences capitalise on the sharing of ideas and on the learning potential of talk. Peer influence, a great stimulus in any learning situation, provides a powerful mechanism for the promotion of books of all types. With a great number of children, reading conferences stimulate enormous interest in literature, particularly for enjoyment and relaxation, but also as a means of exploring their world. I am always over-joyed when I hear snippets of children's conversations about books they are reading. This desire to share insights and experiences has become a natural part of the children's conversations both inside and outside my classroom.

I am now confident that reading conferences provide scope for children:

- to learn language — both specific to the discussion of literature, and general — in interaction with others
- to learn through language — through reading and discussing ideas
- to learn about language — through immersion in book language and group talk opportunities

As a means of developing children's competence as oral language users, as well as their responses to literature, reading conferences are worth talking about.

Reading Conference Record

Name: _____

Date	Conference: Book/Author/ Theme	Preparation	Participation/ Sharing	Memory Recall	Ability to Reorganize Ideas	Ability to Infer	Judgement & Appreciation of Style, Technique

'Talking in the Writing Conference'

Dian Van Dijk

I have seen the videos. I have read the books. I have worked as a language arts adviser in primary schools and now, back in the school, I have tried to build a classroom where talking is a real and valuable part of learning. Lacking the support of parents or teacher aides, I have found it necessary to teach children more about talking and its purposes than perhaps I would have done if I had felt that each child had an interested adult readily at hand. I've had to develop strategies which ensure that no child is ignored and that everyone has a chance to talk when they need to without over-whelming the reading, writing and listening that is taking place at the same time. The children know that talking during the language workshop is not only acceptable but highly valued, and they have often contributed by sug-gesting or modifying many of the procedures outlined in this chapter. While these refer in the main to my middle school classroom, they also have wider application, having been developed for a class where there are writers whose work is almost unintelligible, others whose spelling is phonetic and others still who show high levels of competence.

Talking is the lesson

Just how much talking takes place and how often varies for each child. At one end of the spectrum are the children who are so totally self-directed that interaction with them is minimal except for the talking that they initiate for particular purposes. They know what they need. At the other end are the children who will sit through the most wonderfully stimulating lessons a teacher could devise on ideas for writing and genre — and then, when the writing folder is opened and the blank page is staring back, it all seems to be for nothing. Or they may start, as Chris did, by writing:

> monkey cum her monkey were are you hes killing monkey they kant find him
> monkey were are you monkey hit the frog king with hes staf

Attending to the conventions first is not the answer; it simply produces:

> 'Monkey, come here! Monkey, where are you?'
> He's killing Monkey. They can't find him.
> 'Monkey, where are you?'
> Monkey hit the Frog King with his staff.

The problems Chris was having with this piece of writing arose because he needed more time and a chance to clarify his ideas before taking pencil to paper. We talked about the television series from which his characters were drawn; about whether readers would need extra background to understand the action taking place; about ordering ideas. As he spoke, I jotted down some of his remarks on his notebook for future reference. His conversation tended to jump around: he would say something and that would spark an idea or refresh his memory. But ideas had to come out first before he could work on the structure. This was more than a conversation. This was *the lesson* — a lesson for Chris in the most meaningful context possible and for purposes that *he* defined.

Much of the time and effort that children put into writing drafts could be better used if there were more opportunities to talk — not just at designated 'conference' times after a piece of writing is under way, but while ideas are being tested and before the writer is fully committed. I believe that the most important talk takes place during the early stages of writing, and that we often push children into writing before they have had a chance to discuss and reflect.

Generally, the first discussions centre on formulating and developing the main idea:

> 'What are you/am I writing about?'
> 'What do you/I want to say in this piece of writing?'
> 'Why are you/am I writing this piece?'

These are the kinds of questions that writers in my class ask themselves and each other. When I am talking about writing with a new group of children, I explain that the issue of what or why a writer wants to write has to be considered first.

The talking that I do in writing conferences mainly covers these four areas:

- reinforcing teaching points already covered in class or group lessons (suggestions for how to handle story structure, characterisation, mood, etc.)

- teaching new strategies appropriate to the expertise of the writer

Children need to talk about ideas, and to talk them through, before they begin to write.

- helping the writer to clarify his or her main idea, or to make a decision about the appropriate genre
- retelling what the writer has drafted with discussion about expanding ideas.

The talking that children do lets them solve problems that could not usually be solved by writing alone. It lets them stand aside from their writing and take a fresh approach. However, the ideas that come out in their conversations are not necessarily ones that appear on paper. Writers are not limited to one medium.

Organisation for talking

The classroom is split into two areas: the quiet writing area, which occupies about two-thirds of the room, and the conference area, which uses one side of the room and some of the space immediately outside. Children may talk when they are in the quiet writing area, but the understanding is that other children must be allowed to work undisturbed, and so here we have mostly short whispered conversations. In the early days I sat between the two areas to ensure that the quiet writing area was serving its purpose and to keep an eye on what was happening in the conference areas. Now I move freely from group to group.

The children have their own work folders. I collect a quarter of them each night from Monday to Thursday so that I get to see everyone's folder once a week. (Monitoring one batch of folders takes only quarter of an hour.) All work is dated and any one page may have several dates on it. If children do not have much writing to show for the day, they write a note beside the date:

15 May   I was checking my spelling and talking to Mark about the report.

16 May   I was looking up frogs at the library.

Our language workshops start with a 10-15 minute focus, usually for the whole class, on some aspect of writing. This is followed by 3 minutes of silent writing or thinking time during which the children get themselves organised and ready for whatever stage of writing they are up to, without interruptions. Next I like to talk to the seven or eight children whose folders I collected the previous day. My opening depends on the child:

'What did you mean to say in this part about...?'

'I see you found a way to get that information about lasers in.'

'What gave you the idea to use this lead?'

Or it might simply be,

'Do you need any help?'

I have found that I can get around this group fairly quickly because I have seen their folders beforehand. The system of monitoring folders and offering immediate follow-up ensures that nobody is ignored. I see every folder and talk to each child during the course of a week.

The rest of the workshop time is free to be spent with any children who need help.

Talking to children about conventions for writing can be very time-consuming, especially when they forget to do the basic checks themselves. To overcome this and to encourage the children to do as much of their own editing as possible, I made some labels on coloured cardboard which the children attach to their final draft with a paper clip:

> **I put a line**
> **under the spelling**
> **I need to check**

> **I put capitals for**
>
> **names and the title**

> **I checked fullstops**
>
> **and capital letters**

These labels are an indication of what the writer has tried to do unaided. When we come to talk about spelling and punctuation, it is easier to see where the problems are.

Types of talking

Who talks? Everyone. We talk with partners, in small groups, large groups and to the tape recorder. Discussions may be initiated by me or by the children.

I began using a tape recorder to help slower and less fluent writers to get their ideas down, but we have since found that some of the best results have come from children talking with a partner about aspects of their writing with the tape running. Talking through their ideas allows children to do a lot of the early drafts of a piece of writing in their heads. It's much quicker and allows for more flexibility. The tape recorder can also act as a bank for the writer's ideas, which are then called up as needed. Sometimes children will tire of writing before their ideas have been fully explored and so they use the tape recorder to complete their work. (Even the writer of a seventeen-page saga can still have a lot more to say.)

In teacher-child conferences interaction is always two-way. Sometimes I do much of the talking. Sometimes the writer does. Writing has a lot to do with solving problems and so we work on them together:

> 'Yes, I can see you've got a problem there.'
>
> 'Have you thought about...?'
>
> 'Maybe we should take another look at....'

A considerable amount of the time I spend talking with individual children is still taken up by those who have difficulty writing. They seem

Partners use a tape recorder to remind themselves of ideas explored earlier.

unable to hold all the ideas in their head and write at the same time. It is too much of a load for them. But when they *draw* the battlefield, or cave, or treehouse, or monster, they realise the characters and the setting before they even start writing. The best time to get the talking going is between the picture and the words.

TEACHER: What do you want to write about?

DANIEL: Um... I don't know. He's shooting him.

TEACHER: Is the main thing you want to write about the battle between these people?

DANIEL: He's trying to get away with the treasure.

TEACHER: Who is this? And who is this?

Daniel could not conceive an introduction for his writing because he had not made the step of asking himself whether anybody else needed to understand what he understood already.

Any gap between what is in your head and what goes down on the page is best explored through talking.

Much of the talking that I do with children is intended to serve as a model to help them in their discussions with each other. In the beginning, children use a three-point approach in responding to a partner.

- They comment on where they feel there is too much information.

  'Do you need all that part there about what the bunyip had for dinner?'

- They comment on where they feel there is not enough information.

  'It just says, "The firemen put the fire out". Do you think you should tell more about that part?'

- They ask a question.

  'How did the cat get into the fridge in the first place?'

Small group conferences often take place towards the end of draft writing when one of the children wants an audience response. The writer might withhold the ending and ask the group to guess what happens. She might read the piece without revealing the title and ask for suggestions. She might ask someone to retell the story, describe one of the characters or recall some information. It takes time to teach children how to respond. I do it through direct teaching, by modelling, and by getting children or even another teacher to role-play a good conference partner.

Functions of talking

Talking serves many purposes. We use it as a stimulus to help children choose topics and forms for writing. Writers extend their ideas as they bounce suggestions off each other. Reworking is easier when you talk it over with a partner or group. Talking sets a direction for the piece of writing. Children often have the words and the thoughts but lack the structure. Through talking, they develop the ability to put their ideas together in a logical sequence.

Talking can also be a great aid to presentation, as demonstrated by this encounter overheard between a colleague and his Year Six student.

> KAREN: Sir, I don't know what to draw for an illustration on this page.
>
> MR K: How many images can you find in the writing here?
>
> KAREN: *(after re-reading the page)* Three.
>
> MR K: What are they?
>
> KAREN: Well, there's Daddy looking for the matches because the fuse is gone. There's the dark house and there's the baby crying.
>
> MR K: Which image do you want your readers to see?
>
> KAREN: I think — the baby crying.

Talking extends a writer's options and speeds up the selection process. If something is not quite working, I, or another child, might say, 'Do you like the idea that the dragon might do this, or he could do this, or this...?' and the writer makes suggestions too. It's really up to the writers. It doesn't so much matter what they choose, or even whether they like their original idea — it's more important that they come to realise that they have choices to make and learn how to discover these choices through talking.

Talking goes on

Focussing on talking, which is an easier form of expression than writing for children, takes the pressure off young writers. They see their ideas valued first and their perception of what writing is all about changes. As speaking and listening skills develop, we see them applied outside the writing workshop. Children talk over their problems for a maths activity. They ask better questions. They know what they want when they research in science because much of what they need to know has been talked about and sorted out first. The children are a step ahead because talking has added an extra dimension to their learning.

'Exploring Talk in a Year Five Classroom'

Steve Stronach

I am a Year 5 teacher with an interest in children's talk in everyday situations in the classroom. I'm not simply interested in how well children speak or in how correct their grammar happens to be. What interests me most is how they use talk for reporting, conferencing, small group work, presenting, and a myriad of other purposes.

Recently I set out to document the range of talk that was occurring in my class of twenty-eight children. I tape-recorded 'talk' randomly throughout the day and labelled its purposes afterwards. I also kept a log in which I noted details of contexts and other anecdotal observations. I wanted to find answers to three questions:

- Does my classroom reflect my beliefs about language learning and teaching.?

- Who is doing the talking in the classroom?

- How can I use what I find out to support children's learning?

Does my classroom reflect my beliefs?

I believe that children should be encouraged to use a wide range of spoken genres. They need to know the most effective way to talk in particular situations. To help children understand this and gain the necessary skills, I believe that I must model particular genres frequently and provide many, many opportunities for children to use the appropriate language so that they feel familiar with it. However, I also believe that children learn from each other.

I believe that children will be most successful if they are provided with genuine purposes for talking in a focussed context. I believe too that it is important to monitor each child's language, both to understand what is going on in the classroom and as a base on which to build support for that child.

What did my tapes tell me?

I found that the children were immersed in oral and written language. They were using the kinds of language I modelled. In addition, children were modelling language for other children.

I was pleased to note that I did demonstrate how to use language. I did provide genuine purposes for speaking, although I tended to focus on whole class activities rather than small group interactions. I did create focussed learning episodes, but often the talk that occured was related to print. I confirmed that activities were most successful when routines had been set up.

I also grew more aware of a number of other issues. For instance, while I knew that different contexts for talk have different conventions, it became more apparent that children need help to master them — the skills are *not* 'natural'.

My major concerns seemed to be the child's self-confidence, ability to take risks, to accept responsibility and to make a commitment to the task.

As I talked with other teachers about what I was observing, I realised that we were examining moral issues concerning power in the classroom. Reflection often led to discussions on children's rights. (Very interesting!)

I also soon realised that I needed more information on language development and on how to analyse language. In particular, I've had to sharpen up my understanding of grammar in order to be able to describe, discuss and support what children are doing.

I confirmed for myself that I need to know what children can do if I am to help them make further gains. I've found that sitting in on a small group as an observer, watching all the children while one of them is speaking, and noticing how listeners as well as speakers conduct themselves, is a good way of finding out if the children know what is expected of them.

Although I do not try to evaluate more than one or two children at any one time, I often make anecdotal records for myself about a child. These are useful for keeping up to date with the child's progress and development. However, I don't keep records unless a child has a problem in a particular area or is performing exceptionally well. There is no point in making records and keeping notes that are not going to be needed or read. Teachers have enough to do without creating extra work.

Finally, I believe that by creating this taped opportunity to listen to myself in the classroom, I have learned a great deal more about myself and my teaching.

Who is doing the talking?

When I played the tapes back I was surprised by what I heard. I remember one particular piece of recording where children were presenting projects to the whole class. 'Presenting' as a genre had been modelled by me several times. It had been discussed by the class and some 'rules' had been established:

- Do not interrupt the speaker during the presentation.
- Do not move around the room.
- Listen carefully to what is being presented.

On playing the tape back, the first thing I noticed was that I had interrupted one child four times during a presentation and most children at least once — a classic case of 'Do what I say and not what I do.'

I've also learnt from listening and watching that children take on roles. For example, in small groups one child often takes on the teacher role. I've noted that it is not necessarily the child who is most proficient in the particular area under discussion who takes on that role, but rather the child who is most articulate. Being able to use language appropriate to the genre is definitely an advantage. The danger is that the teacher may think that because a particular child is taking charge and guiding the group, he or she is the group expert in that area. Often this is not the case.

On one occasion, for instance, I taped a small group working on the probability of numbers appearing on dice. Lucy was doing all the teacher talk — organising and advising in this fashion:

> 'You take the dice... You got 6... Yeah, but you have... Where are you up to?...'

I naturally assumed that this child (who incidentally took up 75% of talk time) would perform very well when she came to write down her results. However, when I checked the work, I discovered that the 'teacher', who was very good at keeping the group on task, was not particularly competent with probability!

I noted this again in a small writing group which was supposed to be conferencing the work of all the writers. In this case the best speaker had taken the limelight and the other two didn't really get a look in. The interesting thing was that although the most vocal of the three was not the best writer, the other two, quieter children were prepared to sit back and listen.

I now try to ensure that *all* children in the class obtain experience and exposure, not just those who are the most confident and outspoken.

I would think that the most common genre in use in the classroom is the whole class lesson taken by the teacher. I admit that I use it on a regular basis. But from taping such lessons, I have discovered that unless I am very careful, 90% or more of the talk time is taken up by me. The only chance the children have to contribute to the lesson is when they are asked direct questions — Where?, Why?, etc. They are allowed very little room to contribute constructively. For children who are quiet or shy, constant exposure to this type of lesson may be detrimental. For these reasons I am now trying to reduce my use of whole class lessons.

How can I use what I found out?

As teachers we have certain obligations towards the children we teach. We are expected to teach them to add, subtract, read and write, speak correctly and so on. We also have an obligation to help them become proficient in as many speaking and listening situations as possible. We need to give them the chance to work with different groups, sometimes as listener and sometimes as group organiser.

Obviously some children easily learn and adapt to the 'rules' for particular language situations. Others, especially those who prefer to take a 'back seat', need to be exposed to *all* the language roles involved in a particular context. We need to model and discuss the necessary skills regularly, and then give the children opportunities to practise them in a one-to-one situation before they face a large group.

I discovered that I had in my class a group of six or seven children who were poor at putting together a project, and especially poor at presenting it, although they were neither lazy nor uninterested. I put them together in a group and we spent some time discussing what they thought their weak points were and how they could be improved. Most of them decided that their problem was that they could not 'give the talk'. However, what they came to realise was that by discussing this within the group they were already learning the skills required to present ideas.

I then suggested that they should, as a group, present a project to the class. To ensure that the presentation went well, each child practised presenting his or her section to the group and me first. The whole exercise took some time, but their final presentation of the project to the class was creditable. This experience reinforced one of the lessons of the tapes: many children need models and frequent opportunities for practice if they are going to master the skills required for talking in a variety of situations.

Conclusion

Children derive satisfaction from being able to talk effectively. Being able to converse fluently and use appropriate 'context rules' are expected in our society. It is up to us as teachers to help children become effective talkers. Along the way we'll probably find that we enjoy listening to them.

'Talking with Aboriginal Children'

John Dwyer

'What name you call?'

I turned to find that my questioner was Norman, a six-year-old Aboriginal boy, all smiling eyes and white teeth.

'He looks bright enough,' I thought, 'what a pity he can't speak properly.'

It was my first day as principal in a school in an Aboriginal community and I had brought with me to the position a range of unchallenged attitudes and expectations about Aborigines.

Attitudes and expectations

On the basis of this snippet of speech I had already made a judgement about Norman's language development and, probably without even being aware of it, I had linked this language judgement to a further one about his general ability and intelligence.

Sadly these kinds of judgements are often made about Aboriginal children. Sadly, because the implications of teacher expectations for both teacher and taught are now widely understood.

If as a teacher I have low expectations of a child's performance, my expectations are constantly confirmed for me not so much by the child's actual performance as by the ways in which I selectively perceive that performance. At the same time my expectations are somehow transmitted to the child, who may accept them as confirming his or her own low self-concept and consequently perform 'down' to my expectations, thus creating a vicious and self-perpetuating cycle.

But what of my initial judgement? Surely Norman's utterance was evidence of poor language performance? Yet to sustain such a judgement I would have to be able to define the criteria on which it was made.

Meaning: Norman's sentence was just as meaningful as if he had said, 'What is your name?' or, 'What are you called?'

Function: His sentence was functional. It achieved its purpose of attracting my attention and initiating a contact. I clearly understood it to be a question requiring a response.

Form: Well, at least I can claim that his grammar was incorrect. Or can I? Again, to make such a claim I need to define 'correct grammar'. The most I can say about the utterance is that it does not obey the grammar rules of Standard Australian English.

In fact, the program that I had been appointed to implement was based on a research-derived understanding that many Aboriginal children speak a non-standard but rule-governed dialect of English, often loosely labelled Aboriginal English. These Aboriginal children do speak 'grammatically', but their grammar is different from that of Standard Australian English. The research had shown, for instance, that Aboriginal English generally omits the various forms of the verb 'to be', often doesn't use the past tense marker 'ed', and often does not invert question forms.

Hence Norman's 'What name you call?' was grammatically correct in terms of Aboriginal English.

Testing what, and with what effect?

'But,' you might say, 'you're splitting hairs. Years of language testing have proved that Aboriginal children are generally well behind white children in language development and language performance.'

I wonder? I wonder what tests really prove. For that matter, I wonder what many tests really test. Let's consider some test items. You might like to give your answers as you read.

dog yuk pup yerk cat yuk _____.

Obviously the answer is 'kitten'. Well, perhaps it isn't so obvious. It would have been if I had written 'Dog is to pup as cat is to _____.' You would have realised that I was trying to test your understanding of a relationship between adult animals and their young. But remember that many Aboriginal children do not use forms of the verb 'to be', so that the unusual Standard Australian English form 'is to' would sound as nonsensical to them as 'yuk' did to you. Hence this apparently simple relationship test may include a major syntax problem for them.

Conductor is to orchestra as teacher is to _____.

Let's ignore the syntax problem for a moment and just look at the vocabulary demand of this item. I wonder how many Aboriginal children, especially those living in the more isolated parts of Australia, have any experience of conductors and orchestras (perhaps they may have heard of a conductor on a train or bus but this knowledge won't help them here). An item like this may work against the Aboriginal child because of its cultural irrelevance.

During the day we're at school, at night we're _____.

Well, surely this is more straightforward. Everyone should know about day and night and school and home.

But again the syntax may distract Aboriginal children. Remember, they may not use forms of the verb 'to be', so that they may very well hear 'we're' as 'wear'. This explains why many of them respond to this test item with 'pyjama'.

'During the day we're at school' — yes, that's right. 'At night wear'— oh, he's not asking about school. He's asking what we wear at night. That's easy, 'pyjama'. (By the way, the omission of the plural 's', and of many 's' verb forms and 's' possessive markers are other examples of rule-governed differences between Standard Australian English and Aboriginal English.)

The roof of the house is made of (wood, tiles, paper).

You realise that you are supposed to select the 'correct' response from those given. (Interestingly, it is possible that any of these could be correct, depending on where in the world the house is.) Many Aboriginal children, applying their real world knowledge, ignore all the alternatives and answer 'iron', a 'correct' response which fails to score because it ignores the test convention.

I sit on a chair. I sleep on a _____.

This item is similar to the previous one. Many Aboriginal children will respond 'floor', 'blanket' or 'table', all correct in real terms but incorrect in the terms of the test maker, who believes that all people sleep on a bed.

Ears are to hear with. Eyes are to _____.

How do you react to the Aboriginal child who responds 'Yes'?

'Ears are to hear with.' That's right. 'Eyes are to (two).' Oh! He's not interested in ears. He's really talking about eyes. We have two eyes, so 'Eyes are two.' Yes, that's right.

Or to the Aboriginal child who responds 'big'. 'Eyes are too big.' This was a common response in my school, where staring at someone was considered insulting and provocative: ' 'e big-eyeing me' was a justification frequently offered by a child who had, for no apparent reason, thumped another child.

What should you do if you cut yourself?

I guess that most of you would suggest some form of first aid. Many Aboriginal children, failing to note a distinction in meaning between 'should' and 'would' (remember the research finding about the verb 'to be'), respond 'Bleed' — a perfectly appropriate response if the question had been, 'What *would* you do if you cut yourself?'

I hope I've given enough examples to make my point. If a number of these items appeared in a standardised test, normed on children speaking Standard Australian English, then the 'reading age', or whatever age the test was supposed to be measuring, would be severely deflated for the Aboriginal child, despite the fact that all the alternative responses given are logical.

On the basis of these results it would be valid to say that the Aboriginal child does not have a sound grasp of Standard Australian English, but it would not be valid to go beyond this and say that the test results prove that the child has poor language development. And certainly there is no justification whatever for going even further and claiming that these results prove that the child is 'dumb'.

We need to be very much aware of the language demands of any test. We also need to be aware of the importance of the child's attitude to testing itself. (This is often called 'test set'.) Children from Australian mainstream culture usually have a positive, competitive 'set' towards testing. They are used to being asked questions. They understand the rules of the game. 'Right' means guessing what the teacher wants and giving that response. Many Aboriginal children come from a cultural background where 'wh__' questions are not commonly used and where there is an expectation that questions, when asked, are asked for real purposes, as a genuine seeking for information. Accordingly they may see little point in providing an answer that doesn't accord with their experience, or in providing a response to someone who clearly knows the answer to the question already.

If we are to work successfully with Aboriginal children, we need to do more real listening to their responses and provide opportunities for more real discussion. We need also to interpret their responses with care.

Consider this mathematics question:

Is 2 + 3 bigger than 4?

We know from research that many Aboriginal children do not use the comparative forms 'bigger' or 'bigger than'. So, faced with a question like this, they encounter a language dilemma which is quite distinct from the mathematical concept being tested. If they choose to guess and say 'Yes', the teacher is likely to think that they understand the concept. If they guess 'No', the teacher may respond by focussing on the mathematical concept, failing to realise that the problem lies in the language being used.

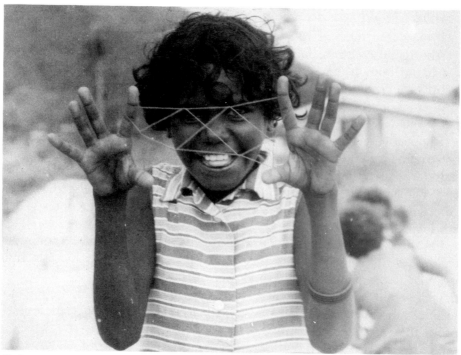

String games often tell a story. Aboriginal children enjoy sharing these stories with their teacher. At the same time the teacher can use the string patterns to introduce 'school-related' ideas such as naming and counting shapes, describing comparative sizes, or defining and clarifying concepts like perimeter or area.

I have vivid memories of a case of this sort. I walked into a classroom one day to find the teacher at the limit of her patience with Kurt, who seemed to have no understanding of the concept of equality. To ease the tension I decided to take over, only to find that soon I too was getting frustrated and angry. Then I had a stroke of luck. I made one 'train' of 4 blocks and two of 2 blocks each. I placed the trains side by side so that the 2 + 2 train sat beside the 4 train.

'There,' I hissed, 'look at that. What can you tell me about the two sets of trains?'

Kurt looked at me with surprise at my obvious stupidity.

'Oh. They tie,' he said.

Suddenly it became obvious that he did have an understanding of the concept. The difficulty had been that his teacher and I expressed that concept through the word 'equal' while he used the word 'tie', a word we would have used if we had been talking about runners who had reached the finishing line simultaneously.

As I said, I was lucky, although Kurt's teacher still thinks I'm a wizard. Actually, any smugness that I might have felt was dissipated some months later when I visited another school and found a teacher in a similar difficulty. Giving him a 'let me help you' look, I turned to the child and said, 'They're equal, aren't they? They tie.' He gave me a contemptuous look and replied, 'No. They level.'

Language difference, not language deficit

In talking with Aboriginal children, then, we need to realise we are dealing with language differences rather than language deficit. Sometimes these differences occur in the grammar forms being used, and I have already mentioned some of the more common examples.

As part of the testing for our program, the research team had used elements of the *Illinois Test of Psycholinguistic Abilities* (Kirk et al. 1968). One of the subtests measures the child's ability to make an automatic grammatic closure. In response to the cue, 'I see one dog. Now I see two _____', you will automatically respond 'dogs'. The cue, 'Today I go to town. Yesterday I _____ to town', will generate the response 'went'.

The Aboriginal children's results on this sub-test (summarised below) caused us concern until we realised that the consistency of the 'wrong' responses was evidence of the fact that grammatic closure was occurring, but in terms of a different grammar.

SYNTACTIC FORM BEING TESTED	EXAMPLE	% STD AUST ENGLISH RESPONSE	
		LOCATION A	LOCATION B
(i) plural noun	dog - dog*s*	36%	16%
(ii) plural noun	dress - dress*es*	10%	0%
(iii) possessive noun	belonging to John - is John*'s*	19%	6%
(iv) comparative adj	big - bigg*er*	10%	9%

One way of interpreting the results for item (i) is to say that within these two groups of Aboriginal children, 64% and 84% respectively were 'wrong'. Another way is to note that of those 64% and 84%, almost all made a closure which omitted the final 's' — 'I see one dog. Now I see two dog' — thus confirming the Aboriginal English grammar 'rule' that the singular and plural forms of these words are the same, the plurality of the latter being indicated by the word 'two'.

Similarly, most of these Aboriginal children responded to items (ii) and (iii) by omitting the final 's' (or 'es').

Although in item (iv) these Aboriginal children did not use the Standard Australian English form 'bigger', they were able to express this concept by elongating the vowel; in fact, the wider their eyes and the longer the vowel, the bigger the object: ' 'e big one. 'e b-i-i-i-g one.'

While these grammatical differences may be striking to ears tuned to hearing Standard Australian English, generally they present few problems in terms of the sharing of meaning.

Sometimes the differences occur in the vocabulary being used. My examples of the use of 'equal', 'tie' and 'level' belong here. Another example that stays in my memory, because of the effect it had on the child's self-concept, occurred when I visited a school as an inspector.

At morning talk an Aboriginal child was excitedly giving her news.

'My uncle in jail. 'e steal too much money.'

Perhaps the teacher was concerned about how the inspector might react to this sort of news. She looked at me across the child's head and said in a disparaging voice, 'I don't know. It seems as if it's all right if you steal, just as long as you don't steal too much.'

The child, unsure of what the teacher meant, but aware that it wasn't positive, looked crestfallen and subsided into silence.

What the teacher hadn't understood was that in that particular Aboriginal community, the term 'too much' was used in the way that a Standard Australian English speaker would use 'a lot of'. Children who told their teacher, 'I got too much pencil' (meaning 'I have a lot of pencils') were often surprised to be told, 'Oh! Well, put some away then.'

Sometimes these vocabulary differences involve the use of words from an Aboriginal language; sometimes they involve the use of 'old English' words no longer common in Standard Australian English. Children in my school sometimes came to school tired and soon dozed off. Usually they were allowed to sleep. Noting this, others would sometimes pretend to be asleep. Often their attempt to trick the teacher was frustrated by a class-mate who would call out, 'Eh Teacher! 'e *gammin* sleep' (he's *pretending* to be asleep).

Again, while some of these differences can be striking, they create few problems for shared understanding, particularly if teachers seek advice about local usages.

Sometimes the differences occur in the sound system. Teachers whose ears are not tuned to Aboriginal English often find that the rate of utterance, with words seeming to run into each other, can create communication problems. Similarly, non-Aboriginal listeners may have difficulty with the different stress patterns. Many Aboriginal speakers stress all syllables equally, whereas Standard Australian English stresses some syllables and not others, the stressed ones often being those that carry particular grammatical markers which help convey meaning.

It's important to keep in mind that in these cases the problem is really the teacher's rather than the child's. Sometimes, too, the teacher can help create the problem by failing to realise that different pronunciations of

Taking Aboriginal children outside the classroom allows them to teach us about their environment and lifestyle. It provides them with real purposes for talking. It also helps us learn more about their general knowledge and language competence. Such experiences can sometimes be captured on film and used as a stimulus for further talking.

certain sounds are culturally based and do not signal the need for speech therapy. Many Aboriginal English speakers don't make a distinction between certain vowels, so that it is common to hear children saying 'one *mairn*' (man), 'two *mairn*' (men). Because the child pronounces these words in the same way, it doesn't mean that he or she is unable to discriminate their meanings. Actually Aboriginal children are operating with additional sets of homonyms.

We assume that children will distinguish between words like 'rain', 'rein', and 'reign' in context. Similarly there is no reason why Aboriginal children can't discriminate differences in meaning in other sets of words which they pronounce as homonyms, even though this may create some difficulties for their teachers.

Standard Australian English uses a high degree of redundancy to help convey meaning. The utterance, 'Look, there are three birds' has three markers to indicate plurality — 'are', 'three', 'birds'.

Aboriginal English speakers might express the same idea like this: 'Look dere (there). Dere tree (three) bed (birds).'

Plurality is signalled only in the word 'three'. 'Are' as part of the verb 'to be' has been omitted, and no distinction in sound has been made between singular 'bird' and plural 'birds'.

By the way, the substitution of a 'd' sound for 'th' (dere/there) and of a 't' sound for 'th' (tree/three) are also common sound system differences rather than examples of failure which require therapy. Although there may be some cases where these sound differences create problems of understanding for the child, it is important to be aware of and accept them in cases where the child is clearly discriminating differences in meaning.

This could have particular significance for beginning readers who are developing a reading 'rule' that you *read* words in the same way that you *say* them. The teacher will accept and praise their rendering of the words '*k*nee' as 'nee', 'of*t*en' as 'offen', and 'lam*b*' as 'lam'. However, if the teacher then criticises their reading of '*h*orse' as 'orse', or of 'b*ir*d' as 'bed' (without realising that these pronunciations are culturally based), it is possible that the children will lose confidence in their developing 'rule' and resort to random guessing rather than 'reading words as they say them'.

At some stage they will need their attention drawn to these differences. But it is important that they are explained to them as differences rather than as errors.

We need to be aware of all of these kinds of differences (grammar, vocabulary, sounds) when we interpret the language performance of Aboriginal children.

Testing — what can we learn from 'errors'?

Part of the research program to which I have referred involved the use of a sentence repetition test. The tester asked the child to listen to a sentence and then repeat it. Because the children were young, the tester would often say, 'I'm going to tell you a story. You listen to the story and then you tell it to me.'

Here are the results obtained from two groups of Aboriginal children on two items in this test.

SENTENCE	% ACCURATE RESPONSE	
	LOCATION A	LOCATION B
We sleep at night.	92%	91%
That's a little bit.	43%	44%

While repetition of the first four-word sentence was fairly accurate, there was a marked falling off in accuracy with the second, although it was of similar length. Our first reaction to this result was in terms of negatives.

'The children have a short attention span.'

'They have middle ear infection and so can't hear what we say.'

'They're careless and don't try.'

'They don't have enough language to be able to repeat the sentence accurately.'

It was only after we listened more closely to the taped responses that we realised what was happening. Instead of 'That's a little bit', we were getting responses such as, ' 'e little bit big', ' 'e little fella.'

Clearly the children had interpreted our instructions literally. They were listening to our 'story' and then telling us theirs in a way which matched it in terms of meaning but not in structure. Rather than language failure or poor language development, they were exhibiting high levels of language skill — the ability to receive a message in Standard Australian English, to interpret its meaning, and then to reproduce that meaning through an Aboriginal English language structure.

This understanding alerted us to the need to think carefully about what we meant by terms like 'correct' and 'error'. Increasingly we found ourselves talking about language that was appropriate in a given context. Rather than seeing 'errors' as bad and to be avoided at all costs, we came to see them as indicators of what the child was learning and as guides to further teaching and learning.

In my role as inspector I recall watching a teacher giving a dictation test to his class.

'He ran his hand down the wall.'

(Later I asked him why that sentence and he told me that he had been concentrating on 'an' words.)

I watched a boy sitting near me write,

e run is han down wall •

(There was no doubt about which punctuation convention was the current focus of attention.)

The teacher's response was to mark the writing thus:

ǝ rǔn ǐs han/down︿wall ■

'Spelling mistake. Spelling mistake. Spelling mistake. Spelling mistake. You left a word out. Write your corrections three times each.'

Sadly this response was not likely to help the child. The teacher had failed to interpret the child's attempts and use them as a springboard.

For example, the omission of the 'h' from 'he' and 'his' can be understood when one remembers that many Aboriginal children don't pronounce this sound. For them it is a silent letter. But the fact that this child had written the 'h' in 'han' (hand) showed that he was aware that this 'silent' letter has a written form (compare Standard Australian English use of 'k' in 'know' or 'b' in 'doubt'). If the teacher had pointed out to the child his 'h' in 'han' and had then shown him that the same letter is written at the beginning of 'he' and 'his', the child could have bridged from his 'old' knowledge to a new understanding.

The 'run' for 'ran' spelling was not a spelling mistake, but resulted from the fact that many verbs in Aboriginal English don't change their form to indicate tense. Thus an Aboriginal English speaker may say, 'Today I run town, yesterday I run town. Tomorrow I run town.' The time element is indicated through the adverbs rather than in the verb tense forms. The child needed to have this explained to him. Merely writing 'ran' three times, without knowing why he should write it in that way, wouldn't have helped him learn why he was 'wrong'.

I could go on. The spelling of 'hand' as 'han' was an attempt to write what the teacher actually said. If you try repeating the sentence aloud, you will probably find that, unless you make a conscious effort, you tend to slide the two 'd's together and say 'han-down'. Finally, the omission of the definite article is once again a common grammatical feature of Aboriginal English. Thus the child didn't leave it out because he forgot it, but because in his grammar it was not necessary.

I am not suggesting that we shouldn't expect and demand that Aboriginal children learn to spell Standard Australian English forms. What I am saying is that we will better help them to do this if we really look at the kinds of 'errors' they make and why they make them.

Aboriginal English — a dialect continuum

Until now I have been talking about Aboriginal English and Standard Australian English as if they were two clearly distinct forms (dialects) of English. In fact the situation is far more complex since we are really dealing with a continuum of usage. Speakers located along the continuum make more or less use of Standard Australian English (SAE) or Aboriginal English (AbE) forms.

Children from a 'close contact' group will use some Standard Australian English and some Aboriginal English forms. Children from a 'remote' group may also use some Standard Australian English forms but will make more use of Aboriginal English forms than the 'close contact' group.

AbE   **SAE**

←——→

'e coat bla John.   Dat John coat.   That's John's coat.
(Aboriginal group   (Aboriginal group
in remote location)   in close contact
                            with SAE speakers)

However, this is still too simplified. We know that as well as controlling a span on the continuum for speech produced, each child also controls an even wider span for receiving language. This means that most Aboriginal English speakers will hear and understand and respond to at least some Standard Australian English forms they do not say, or that they say only rarely.

Let me complicate the situation even more in order to heighten your awareness of the actual language sophistication of Aboriginal children. As well as controlling receptive and expressive spans along the continuum, these children can also adjust their language according to the formality of the situation. Both Aboriginal English and Standard Australian English can be used formally and informally. The style of Standard Australian English that Aboriginal children use when presenting a talk in school will be more formal than the style they use in a personal conversation with their teacher. Similarly, in Aboriginal cultural contexts, Aboriginal English will be used more or less formally depending on the situation.

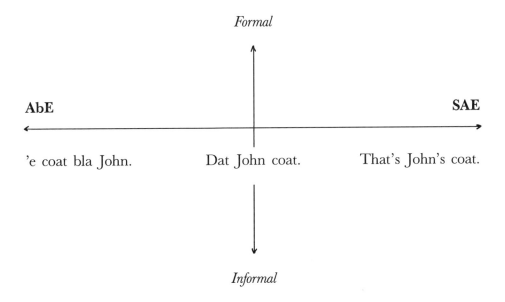

Formal

↑

AbE   **SAE**

←——→

'e coat bla John.   Dat John coat.   That's John's coat.

↓

Informal

Dealing with language difference

Clearly we are not dealing with language deficit. What we are seeing is language difference. Furthermore these linguistic differences are associated with sociolinguistic and cultural differences. Keeping in mind my earlier comments about teacher expectations and self-fulfilling prophecies, we can see that how we deal with these differences is critical for the personal and educational development of the Aboriginal children we teach.

If, as teachers, we see these differences as a 'problem', then our teaching response will be to remediate and compensate, to try to stamp out and replace undesirable language. For the Aboriginal child, the end result of such an approach is likely to be lowered self-esteem.

> 'If you attack my language you attack me, because what I am and what I know and believe and feel are all mediated through language.'

In addition, if we operate from a remediation/compensation position, we operate from a belief in the child's past failure; we build in an expectation of future failure; and at the same time we build in a 'cop-out' for ourselves.

> 'I taught them but they wouldn't (or couldn't) learn.'

On the other hand, if we see these differences as a resource on which further teaching and learning can be built, our teaching response will be to seek to extend the skills that the children already have. We will see ourselves as helping the children to further successful learning, rather than as attempting to remediate past failure. If they fail to learn, we will question our strategies rather than blame their weakness. We will acknowledge past success and build in expectations of future successes.

As a result the children will know that their language is valued and, therefore, that they are valued. They will grow as people and as learners.

'Talking When English Is a Foreign Language'

Betty Murray

How embarrassing! After five years of earnest endeavour, after endless recitations of French verb conjugations, vocabulary and useful phrases, I was entirely unable to make myself understood when lost in Paris. The French of the French didn't sound remotely like mine. They had many chuckles at my expense. There were some who were annoyed and many who shouted instructions as though I were deaf. I felt stupid and gave up the effort. As a result I saw far more of Paris on foot than I'd bargained for. Perhaps you've had similar experiences.

What had gone wrong with my French learning? My failure certainly wasn't related to any inability to learn language. I've learnt English readily, and have even learnt a couple of other less well known languages adequately. I believe that the explanation lies rather in the conditions of language learning listed by Brian Cambourne (1984, 1987). When I studied French in school these conditions were not recognised, and so my limited competence is not surprising.

Torres Strait background

Children learning English in the Torres Strait Islands are in almost the same situation as the one confronting me when I tried to learn to speak French. They do not hear English spoken around them. There has been little expectation that they will learn to use English fluently, and children especially have few opportunities to use the language with native English speakers. In fact, the *only* place in the community in which they may regularly hear and speak English is the school, where it is, officially at least, the language of instruction.

None of the linguistic supports of the surrounding English-speaking community which exist for most ESL children in Australia exist for these children. They are not immersed in the sounds, meanings and culture of English. It is up to the school to provide the reasons and supports for the demanding task of learning to speak English.

Although English has been taught in Torres Strait schools for a century, there is little evidence of it. However, there are valid reasons why these children seldom use English, including:

- the isolation of the communities from the English-speaking Australian mainland
- a preference for the use of other languages
- the teaching methods and English competence of the teachers.

Torres Strait Islanders speak two or more languages indigenous to the region: the languages of the home, ceremonial functions and local trade. English is required only when dealing with English speakers and children rarely have to do that. In addition, a growing awareness of the Torres Strait languages as markers of the people's 'nationhood' makes English less valued.

Torres Strait Islander teachers staffing the schools have varying degrees of proficiency in English and find it difficult to teach any English beyond what is written in textbooks. Until recently they used teaching materials based on repetitive drills which made little or no sense either to them or their pupils. Sometimes these drills could go horribly wrong, as when I heard one class echoing for 15 minutes, 'Yesterday, I buy five apple.' Certainly the English the children were practising was utterly irrelevant to the interesting world they were exploring. For them English was dead.

A new program

In the early 1980s I was asked to lead a team to develop a new English language program for Torres Strait schools. This had to be a program which could operate within the cultural situation I have described. It was intended to:

- help children develop functional skills in English
- take account of the isolation of the schools
- support the teachers in becoming more fluent in Standard Australian English
- provide inservice education in appropriate teaching methods
- provide content and supporting resources for teachers which would both sustain the unique cultural background of the children and introduce the culture of the language they were learning.

Torres Strait Islander children have a rich and unique cultural background. Important cultural activities become part of the fabric of the school program.

On these demands was superimposed the need to excite the children to the point of engagement with the task.

The work of Warwick Elley (1982) and Brian Gray (1984) led to the adoption of two basic notions.

- First, children had to become involved in real exploration of their world in ways that allowed English to be the valid medium of communication — an approach similar to Gray's 'concentrated encounters'.

- Second, books would be used as the stimulus for these explorations and as the scaffolds for teachers' and students' language growth.

The major premise on which the Torres Strait English program rests is that language is for communication. Consequently the major focus of the program has shifted from the form of the language to the children, their interests, their levels of maturity and their natural language learning abilities.

The teacher's role has also changed dramatically, from being an instructor of language forms to being a sharer of new experiences and a supporter in the child's exploration and explanation of his or her world. The task of the teacher has become genuine negotiation of meaning through the medium of English where this is appropriate.

MEANING MATTERS
and
SENSE IS EVERYTHING

are the organising principles. The spoken form of language is regarded as primary, and the intent of the program is represented in the diagram below.

*common experience shared through senses, story, pictures, song, chanting, chatting, telling stories, testimony of past experience, role play, drama

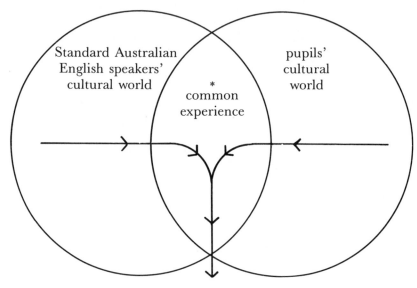

new experience shared

Initially the teachers found it difficult to move away from their formal presentation because the new approach made far greater demands on their limited English proficiency. However, concurrently with the introduction of the new program, English-speaking principals were appointed to the schools and they provided everybody with models of English. The teachers also learned to capitalise on the visits of English speakers to the communities. The amount of genuine interaction in English increased noticeably, and with it came confidence and competence. Schools became talking places and much more of the talk was in English.

Examples of content

The Torres Strait English Program consists of work units and supporting teacher inservice materials. The seven work units for each year level are comprehensively prepared and packaged with all the required supporting resources. Evaluation materials are also included. The extract overleaf from a Year Three unit illustrates the type of materials supplied.

The use of repetitive texts in the beginning years provides fun ways of learning and using English structures. Parents and other community members soon become familiar with the characters and language of the texts used in the early units as children chant along the streets,

> 'Jumping here, jumping there. I can jump everywhere.'

Commercially published texts are supported by texts produced at the Far Northern Schools Development Unit. This local production focuses on the introduction of traditional Torres Strait stories in English translations and on materials which explain mainstream culture to children to whom it is quite foreign. The shared book approach is used extensively to provide opportunities for the children to hear spoken language, to discuss their own related experiences, to make predictions and to use the language of the texts as a model as they express their own ideas and experiences. They seek meaning and learn much more than the conventions of print (although they do this as well). Negotiation of these texts brings the wider world into their shared experiences.

The general structure of the units looks like this.

The real thing →	Chat about →	Consider →	Decide →	Share
books	what is happening	what this shows	response/	new
pictures	to whom		action	experience
albums	when	what we/they		
films	where	need to		
excursions		understand		
community events	how this compares with events in our/ their lives			

The shared-book methodology employed can be illustrated with Hazel Edwards' story *There's a Hippotamus on Our Roof Eating Cake*. The main themes are the seeming unfairness of family rules and the desire for a world in which children might do as they wished. A secondary theme is that of approved and disapproved behaviours.

In presenting the book, the teacher leads the children through the routinised structure.

The real thing (book) ⟶ Chat about and compare with known ⟶ Identify children's needs ⟶ Decide response/action ⟶ Share new experience.

Language Focus: The children should be better able to

*   Describe the physical appearance of turtles.

    eg. *It's got very big flippers and a hard shell.*

*   Describe the behaviour of turtles.

    eg. *She's digging a hole in the sand to make a nest.*

*   Describe changes in the appearance of turtles.

    eg. *Its shell is a little bit bigger.*

Objectives: The children should be learning to

*   Talk about a story they've listened to.

*   Retell a story.

*   Use a story map to retell a story.

*   Dramatize a story.

*   Write factual information (non-fiction).

SUGGESTED ACTIVITIES FOR **TURTLES**

Suggested Time   3 Lessons

	Resources Needed
Begin with **Shared Book Experience.**	*The Smallest Turtle.*

* Talk about - why the turtle leaves the nest.
      - where the other turtles have gone.
      - the words the turtle hears in his head.
      - the other animals and places the turtle passes, and what happens there.
      - how he feels when he reaches the sea.	

* Read the story again.	

	Resources Needed
Make a **Story Map.**	Blackboard Coloured chalks.
* Get the children to slowly tell the story again. Make sure they do this in detail.	
* As the children talk about what happened next; sketch it in on the board. eg. draw the nest of eggs; mark in the path the turtle took; draw the shiny grey rock; draw the big black beetle etc.	
* With each sketch, ask the children to suggest a few words to summarize what happened there. Write this in. (see the diagram in "Chickens.")	
* Using the map to help, get the children to tell the story again, by themselves.	

	Resources Needed
Dramatize the story	*The Smallest Turtle.*

* Select children to be - the turtle.
      - a shiny grey rock.
      - big black beetle.
      - a tree with twisty roots.
      - prickly grass.
      - a spider.
      - a sleepy lizard.
      - a big green leaf.
      - gulls.
      - crabs.
      - seaweed.
      - shells.
      - stones.
(In smaller classes, children might have to be two or three different characters.)	

* Read the story again, giving time for the children to play their parts.	

Shared Book Experience. (Ask somebody who knows a lot about turtles to join you for this lesson eg. someone who worked for Applied Ecology.)
 	
*   Read the story.
 	
*   Talk about - where turtles lay their eggs.
              - how they dig the nest.
              - how you can tell where a turtle nest is.
              - how they lay the eggs, when, how many, how often.
              - how the baby turtles hatch out.
              - how they know which way to go to get to the sea.
              - dangers for the baby turtle.
              - what they do once they get to the sea.
              - what they eat.
              - how long they take to grow to full size.
 	
*   Read the story again.
	The Turtle
	A guest who knows about turtles.

Resources Needed

Writing Non-Fiction.
 	
*   Display the set of pictures.
 	
*   Talk about what is happening in each of these.
*   Use the negotiated text approach, and write *"The Life Story of a Turtle"*, based on these pictures.
    Tape or clip each picture onto a blank sheet of paper
    You can 1) all write the whole story.
        or 2) divide the class into 6 groups, and give each a
                different page to work on.
 	
*   Read the story again when the book is finished.
 	
*   Get the children to read this book to another class.
	Set of 6 pictures of
	butcher's paper
	Felt pens
	Tape or paper clips
	Stapler.

ADDITIONAL ACTIVITIES

* Read poems to the children.	"Road Fellows" p 233 "The Little Turtle" p 115 in *Childcraft:* *Poems and Rhymes.*

ACTIVITIES THAT YOU SUBSTITUTE

This routine generates a great deal of talk and eventually leads to a shared understanding of:

- family and cultural mores
- the fact that rules exist in society and families and that breaking them may lead to punishment
- the place of imagination in our private worlds
- the specific language of the book.

Discussion could centre on such questions as:

'What rules existed in this family?'

'Are they the same as those in your family?'

'Can we make a list of what's approved or disapproved of in your families?'

Some language functions arising naturally would be:

- describing
- questioning
- giving directions
- warning
- prohibiting.

The language focus would then be on such structures as:

'You mustn't....'

'If you (ride your bike on the road) you might (get run over).'

'Why can't I...?'

Suitable responses to the story could be:

- telling a similar story or writing a similar book reflecting the personal experiences of class members
- reminiscing, e.g. 'I remember the time when...'
- singing songs appropriate to the theme or incorporating language functions related to the theme
- researching/describing animals, e.g. hippos
- role play
- preparing a list of rules for the classroom.

Parents and other community members are encouraged to participate in the sharing of these experiences. This ensures that the school does not become distanced from the community and that the children's own cultural mores are supported and valued.

Children visiting the fire-station: excursions like this are another way of involving the school with the community and sharing experience.

Just how much and how quickly children learn when they are engaged in using language for genuine purposes was demonstrated one day when I was visiting the Year 3 classroom of Louise Carothers on Thursday Island. I'd failed to see a guinea pig in a picture in the book I'd been reading. Henry, a seven-year-old who speaks English only at school, enthusiastically pointed it out to me,

'There it is! See over there! It's very well camouflaged.'

To say I was surprised would be a major understatement. To me this utterance was almost miraculous. The precision of use was amazing — and his confidence even more so.

Restrospect

The program I have been describing was written to meet the special needs of children in Torres Strait schools, children such as Henry. However, I am confident that its underlying rationale and the kinds of resources, activities and techniques that it employs have much wider application.

I asked Louise, now at a school on the mainland, but still using the materials and methods with her English-speaking students, to comment on her experiences on Thursday Island — her first experience of teaching non-English-speaking children. I asked her to share her thoughts on why her students used English so confidently and so correctly.

> *I believe the single most important strategy for a teacher to practise is to be a good listener. By this I mean **genuinely** listen to the children. If a child comes to speak, face him, put down the work you are doing and give him your whole attention. Remember to follow up on the conversation at some later date. In this way children see themselves as valued members of the special community of the classroom.*
>
> *Children should be encouraged to become good listeners too. This is not difficult with Torres Strait Island children, where the passing of information by word of mouth is the norm.*
>
> *It is essential that the classroom becomes a talking place. Talk about everything. In our classroom we had 'Islands' on which we sat to chat. These were only woven mats on the floor but they were very important places to us all....*
>
> *Unfortunately, we can often underestimate what the kids will say. I have been astounded many times at what they came out with. They transferred language we used in one situation to others with incredible ease. Because the language was used in understandable contexts they learnt its meaning without any real effort. They actually talked their way to understanding.*
>
> *Although all children are free to speak and are encouraged to do so, it is important not to force them to talk before they are ready. When they do speak, it is important to listen to the meanings. I remember the following exchange between Jack and a teacher.*
>
>> *'We went to Nagi on Saturday, Sir.'*
>> *'How far is away is Nagi, Jack?'*
>> *'Four drums, Sir.'*
>
> *(The journey in a dinghy driven by an outboard motor would take four drums of petrol.)*
>
> *What it really comes down to is that we must have respect for the children themselves. Intellect and interest are not tied to their ability to communicate in English. With respect comes confidence. With confidence comes a willingness to take risks. With risk taking comes learning.*

'Navigating a Sea of Confusion'

Joy Schloss

The 'sea of talk' laps the shores of all lands. Within our country, within our classrooms, we as teachers have opportunities to experience a rich diversity of cultures as we interact with children who have come from overseas. When these children arrive in our classrooms, however, the sea of talk can become, for them, a sea of confusion.

One of the many challenges facing classroom teachers today is how to assist children from non-English-speaking backgrounds (NESB) to achieve their full potential. Classroom teachers shoulder responsibility for supporting both the language development and the continuing academic progress of these children. What happens in our classrooms may well determine whether they sink or swim in our schools, and ultimately in Australian society.

One of the greatest influences on classroom practice is the teacher's own understanding of what language is and how it works as a system for communicating meaning. Teachers who encounter NESB children for the first time can feel reassured when they recognise that learning a second language is similar in many ways to learning one's first language. Many of the principles and strategies that support first language development can be used to support second language learners. Fundamental to both situations is the understanding that *language is learned by using it to interact with others to get something done*. It follows that we need to create in our classrooms a supportive, caring environment where all children, including NESB children, will want to communicate with others for particular purposes.

Without denying that fundamental point, it is important for teachers to recognise that many newly arrived NESB children will need time before they are ready to contribute actively to classroom interactions. Steven

Krashen (1981) identifies three conditions essential to the process of second language acquisition:

- the right to be silent
- a stress-free environment
- comprehensible input.

At the water's edge

Many NESB children entering an English-speaking classroom for the first time spend the first few weeks in almost total silence, watching and listening to all that is going on around them. This period of silence could be likened to someone standing at the water's edge before plunging in. For all children it is a very important stage, as during this time they will be observing and internalising a lot about how English works. They may be doing all or any of the following, and more:

- listening to sounds not heard before
- hearing sounds which resemble known ones but seem to mean something quite different
- becoming aware of the rhythm and intonation patterns of English
- observing a new set of non-verbal signals (such as facial expressions, hand movements, body stance) that may have similar or opposite meanings to those they are familiar with
- watching how different people (teachers, peers, adults) interact socially to express emotions, respect, humour, formality, authority, lack of knowledge
- developing an understanding of routines that are appropriate and expected in this new classroom context
- assigning new words or strings of words to familiar and known items or concepts
- internalising patterns and rules about the new language they are hearing.

NESB children will of course vary in the time spent at this relatively silent stage. Teachers need to be aware of individual needs and respond appropriately, not forcing them to speak before they are ready. At the same time teachers should expect that these children will begin to use English when they are put into situations of *wanting* to interact with peers to get something done. This means, in Krashen's terms, creating a stress-free environment and making sure any input is comprehensible. It is important to recognise that the three conditions which Krashen identified need to occur simultaneously. Teachers should not wait 'until children have some

English' before involving them in meaningful tasks and activities related to work being covered in mainstream content areas. Children need to be involved, and supported in that involvement. Second language acquisition is fostered by a classroom environment where warmth, acceptance and encouragement accompany the invitation to be involved.

Come on in, the water's fine

Just as one can't learn to swim without being in the water, NESB children won't learn the language they need to succeed in school without being engaged in mainstream curriculum content. Supportive teachers will look for ways of involving them in whatever is going on. The learners themselves will want to be part of the class, not separated off to do 'easier' work. They don't need a separate program. Many of them bring to our classrooms successful learning strategies, a high level of conceptual development, and proficiencies in oracy and literacy in at least one other language. Our task as their teachers is to help them continue *learning* at the same time as they are *learning English* and *learning about English*.

Some of the strategies teachers have found effective during the early days, weeks or months include these.

- Assign a 'buddy' to the NESB child. Select a caring, supportive, reliable partner of the same age and sex, who contributes effectively in oral interactions. It's better to select a good talker rather than one of the 'top' students. There is tremendous value in selecting a peer who is at a similar developmental level. Meanings are more likely to be negotiated and contributions shared if one partner is not obviously 'the expert'. Allow the children to sit together and talk about the work at hand, so that the NESB child can copy and imitate the buddy. Encourage the buddy to use natural language and to avoid any patronising attitudes and actions. Be prepared for either partner to reject the system when desired, exploring other options.

- Make good use of music, chants and rhymes where repetitive language is a feature. Use clapping, dance, percussion instruments and actions to highlight the rhythm and sounds of English. It's generally possible to find music material appropriate to class themes or units of work.

- Read aloud books that have predictable language or regular patterns. Use big books so that children can see as well as hear the text. These resources are often more readily available for lower primary levels. Older children can be involved in writing books for younger ones

Make sure that children listening to audio cassettes have enough visual support.

(this needs to be done in small groups so the older children are able to talk about the language needed).

- Use pictures and other visual aids as well as real materials to make links between the language and its meaning. Involve the NESB children in science investigations, field trips, problem-solving activities, craft and any lessons where hands-on work is required. Make use of videos based on class novels. Use filmstrips where the sound can be turned off so that children can make an alternative sound track. (Listening to audio cassettes without the visual support of gestures and facial expressions may be very difficult in an unguided situation.)

- Make good use of whatever bilingual assistance is available within the school or region. At a minimal level this may only involve using a bilingual dictionary. You may be able to get hold of published ones or you can encourage the children to compile their own in content-related sections. If there are other speakers of the same language in the school, arrange times for them to talk together socially and for specific content-based discussions and sharing. When there are two or more of these learners in the same class, give them opportunities to talk in their own language. Even those developing fair competence in English will be able to explore topics to a greater depth in their first language if it is well developed. Remember we want them to continue *learning* as well as learn English. Invite parents, other adults from ethnic organisations, and teachers or students from other schools with the same language background to visit your classroom. Create whatever opportunities you can for talk to occur in all the languages represented in your school. Teachers who take hold of such opportunities not only demonstrate to NESB children that their cultural heritage is recognised and valued, but also give it status in the eyes of others.

- Bilingual assistance can be used to translate books or rhymes into the children's first languages. Sometimes in such translations some of the special oral features of particular texts can be lost; e.g. *Poor Old Polly* (Mesler and Cowley 1980) relies on the rhyming sounds present in the English words used. A translation into Vietnamese results in words that sound quite different, losing some of the special appeal of the text. However, by using the same ideas but different words, a rhyming Vietnamese text can be built up.

- It is important to respond to the children's meaning when they speak rather than stressing correct forms in the early stages. Don't focus on grammatical or pronunciation errors. The NESB children's grammatical forms and accent will come closer to Standard Australian English as they do more listening to and talking with their native-speaking peers. Another danger lies in correcting NESB children's speech patterns when they are forms used by all children in the class (e.g. 'I done my homework, Miss'). They will be confused and upset if they find themselves reprimanded for using the forms they hear around them all the time.

Once our students are immersed in the mainstream, we as teachers need to reflect on our role further. What support do these children need to make the most of their experiences in this sea of talk?

Being there

While recognising that children need to take responsibility for their own learning, teachers have the responsibility for making sure the right conditions prevail in their classrooms.

In the classroom teachers hold the major responsibility for organising curriculum content and resources, and for organising groups of children within the class to facilitate learning. This organisation should encompass the four areas of listening, speaking, reading and writing, and adequate thought must be given to each area. Effective interaction in oral activities is difficult to achieve without careful planning by the teacher. Such deliberate consideration is crucial if NESB children are to be meaningfully engaged. Oral interactions are ideal arenas for exploring new topics, sharing tentative ideas and considering possibilities, because the language is constructed jointly. It uses incomplete structures, it provides room for hesitations, it allows meaning to be negotiated through attempts at new language use, and it allows for inaccuracies to be repaired immediately by others.

TRANG: What it is? Ummmm... it a...
HANH: Shark... no, I mean whale. Look, it got this... a... a...
TRANG: What this call, Ben?
BEN: That's the blowhole. Sharks don't have them. Whales do. And dolphins.

NESB children need many opportunities to interact with both bilingual and native English speakers in small groups that maximise their opportunities to use language in a safe environment. The presence of the teacher can often inhibit children, making them hesistant to have a go. A teacher-dominated question and answer 'discussion' with a large group restricts the number of chances a child has to talk.

When planning activities for the classroom, teachers need to consider whether spoken or written activities will in fact necessitate the use of the language desired. It's quite possible to complete some oral tasks without using the key lexical items in the field of study. Because the oral language accompanies the action, children can refer to many items by using pronouns rather than proper nouns:

'Put it here. Quick. Get that... get that one.'

'Then this goes in here.'

While such language is quite appropriate and enables the task to be completed successfully, it does not assist the NESB child to develop knowledge of the content. Other activities may be needed: for instance, recording the experiment with labelled diagrams will ensure the use of some of the key words. These diagrams can then be used to instruct another child (working behind a barrier of some kind) how to carry out the experiment. A variation would be to record the instructions on tape for another group to follow. These changes to the organisation of activities facilitate oral language development *but do not require deviations from normal curriculum content*. Both the native speakers of English and the NESB children benefit because the level of cognitive challenge increases with the necessity to explain, restate, elaborate on or correct the given information.

There will be many factors that influence decisions about how children are grouped in any situation, including at times the children's own choices. For NESB children there will be times when speakers of the same language may benefit from working together in either their first, second

Change the organisation of activities to develop oral language. Here one child has to instruct the other to create a similar vehicle.

or both languages. When groups are made up of speakers from different backgrounds, including native English speakers, teachers need not worry about the 'correctness' of the language models. Children will modify and advance their oral language development by working with others whose competence is only slightly higher than their own. Central to any consideration of groups will be the needs of the children and the purpose of the activity. Each of these will affect the language that results.

Last one in is a...

How do we, as teachers, know that we have created the conditions that have maximised the language and learning potential of our students? Teachers who have only short periods of contact with particular NESB children will perhaps notice only small ripples. Others will observe over longer periods a growing confidence and competence in the children, both inside and outside the classroom. Some of them will have mastered even colloquial English and enter enthusiastically into a wide variety of life experiences where all languages and cultures are valued and respected. They'll be looking for new seas on which to venture out.

'Talking about Teacher Talk'

John Dwyer

Teachers are talkers. We organise classroom talk and we use talk for organising the classroom. We ask questions. We make jokes. Above all, through our talk we transmit our attitudes and expectations to our pupils. We often consider the talk of children. How often do we focus on our own?

Organising talk in the classroom

Teachers talk a lot. It seems that we set out to impose our own definition on the situation by talking most of the time. Studies have shown that for about two-thirds of the time that teachers and pupils are in the classroom someone is talking. About two-thirds of that talk is done by the teacher, and about two-thirds of the teacher's talk is talk for organising (see, for example, Delamont 1976).

Through this talk we exert control over:

- the channels of communication
- how much talk is considered acceptable
- the content of the talk
- the language form
- what constitutes understanding.

Through this talk we also:

- decide and define how we and the children should attract and show attention
- elicit ideas, prompt speakers, provide clues and reject speech
- decide on, define and edit the topic

- elicit and provide examples
- edit and correct language
- provide 'clarification'.

This talk helps us to define the classroom situation and to uphold that definition. Time after time we hammer home taken-for-granted assumptions about appropriate pupil and teacher behaviour (the hidden curriculum).

> 'When we are doing silent reading, we don't have any talk at all. I hope that's clear....'

> 'Yes. Now then Raymond. I don't know what's got into you this morning, but you haven't been in the mood to try hard, have you?'
> Raymond remains silent, head down.
> 'Well! Am I right or wrong?'

Being able to organise classroom talk gives us considerable power. Not only do we control talk, we also control what constitutes knowledge. We control decisions about the relevance of what children say and control when, how and how much they may speak. How we exercise this control may be critical for the creation of a productive learning environment. Thus we may find it useful, and enlightening, to monitor the way we organise classroom talk. Do we organise wisely, sensitively and constructively, or, in pursuing the goals that we regard as important, do we diverge destructively from some or all of the children with whom we interact?

Talk for organising

As well as organising classroom talk, we also use talk for organising the classroom — for establishing and maintaining order and discipline. While we are not completely free agents (the 'school' and the 'community' may impose certain values and traditions), we decide what our expectations and limits of tolerance are. We define these to our class and get them accepted.

If a mismatch occurs between the expectations of children and teachers, it may engender tension. Children need defined parameters within which they can work comfortably. Indeed many children evaluate teachers by looking for firmness, good humour and understanding. They value teachers who 'teach you', who explain, who are interesting, who are fair, and who are friendly. Lack of firmness and not being made to work are often given as reasons for school's being 'boring'.

Thus children expect us to establish negotiated rules. But they also expect us to follow these rules and to behave in ways that harmonise with them.

> *A new class is not a clean slate passively waiting for a teacher to inscribe his will on it. It is an ongoing social system with very definite expectations about*

appropriate teacher behaviour. If these are not confirmed the pupils will protest and the renegotiated patterns of behaviour may not prove to be just what the teacher intended.

(Nash 1976, p. 94)

Closely related to the issue of rules and expectations is the way in which we communicate our commands. The 'successful' teacher portrays the 'persons' present in a situation and provides a context for them. Teachers commonly refer to 'we', 'I' and 'you' as the 'persons' in a situation. The 'successful' teacher uses these 'persons' to help define the situation.

> 'Stop! Stop! This is um — this is important. This is important. Let's clear this up before we go on.' The class is now silent.
> 'Just put your hands down. This is important, Paul. Jennifer is worried about John getting 16 out of 16, because Jennifer thinks John, by getting 16 out of 16 — he'd only get that if he was cheating. I don't give a monkey's whether John gets 2 out of 16 or 16 out of 16. John will know, whatever score he gets, he will know how many he got right — and that's the important thing. If John thinks it's better — it looks better to get 16 out of 16, then, fair enough... if you all want to put 16 out of 16 you can do — but you might just as well have stayed in bed this morning because you're wasting your time and my time.'

This teacher utterance clearly conveys the following definition of the situation.

- There are rules governing our position here, rules which can be explicitly stated.

- The rules affect all of us (the 'we') without distinction.

- My special position (the 'I') is not that I stand above the rules, but that I can interpret the rules to you if you are in doubt about them.

This definition is not simply conjured up for the occasion. Rather it is portrayed as holding for all occasions.

On the other hand the less successful teacher separates the 'we', 'I' and 'you' so that his 'I' cannot be at one and the same time part of the group and its interpreter. Only one 'person' has a clear view of the situation, his 'I', who is not related to the other 'persons' and is thus not accountable to his 'we'.

> 'I wish you'd stop that noise. Don't you know you should be doing sums now? We'll never get finished at this rate.'

In addition his context offers no definition which claims to go beyond the immediate situation. Because he provides no enduring reality, there is likely to be confrontation when his pupils' views of the situation differ from his.

We might find it valuable to monitor how we present these 'persons' and how we establish contexts in which to situate them. In particular, it could be interesting to observe if or when (and why) any particular child is excluded from the 'we' category. Alternatively, it might be interesting to monitor who is included in a child's 'we' and 'you' groups.

Questions in the classroom

As teachers we ask lots of questions, although we rarely make a genuine request for information. I wonder if we realise that to ask a question is to claim a right — the right to impose on a person's time and energy and to initiate or continue an interaction which may be used to reflect on the identity, status and character of those involved.

Thus questions involve attitudes and values as well as requests for action or information. Teachers are on dangerous ground here. Children are well aware that we already know the answers to most of the questions we ask. Questions then become tests. Through them we claim authority in a way which is quite foreign to normal discussion. How questions are asked, and answers dealt with, may be critical for establishing rewarding personal relationships and an environment in which children can learn.

There is a further issue. Because the child is aware that we already know the answer to our question, the problem for the child is to guess what we want and to provide an answer that is 'correct' in terms of being 'acceptable' to us. The child can display ability only if the answer given conforms to our definition of the situation (including our view of what constitutes knowledge). It could be argued that children become successful to the extent that they develop ways of interpreting our talk.

As teachers, we need to be sensitive to the demands we make, and to the messages we transmit, when asking questions and accepting or rejecting answers.

How often do we, failing to get a response, order the child to talk? Sometimes the command may be low-key:

'What do you think about this? I'd like to know.'

Often it is more aggressive:

'Wake yourself up and answer me.'

The conventions for the use of low-key or aggressive commands are sensitive to the relative status of the speaker and the listener. We need to become more aware of the extent to which we base our question/order behaviour on our status position.

And what of our common teacher habit of repeating children's answers — something which rarely happens in everyday conversation? Such repetitions can be seen as patronising. In any case, they frequently close off discussions.

Consider the following brief classroom interchange. Note how this teacher's repetitions limit the chance of any sustained discussion. In fact, halfway through, she actually interrupts the child to repeat an answer and to ask a further question which the child has already begun to answer.

> MISS S: What do you recognise in the map?
> RUTH: Miss, I recognise Selby Road.
> MISS S: You recognise Selby Road. Who lives in Selby Road?
> RUTH: Miss! Miss! Patricia used to live there but she moved. She went —
> MISS S: She moved. Where did she go to?
> RUTH: She went to Wood Green.
> MISS S: Wood Green. Which school does she go to now?
> RUTH: I don't know.

(Perhaps Ruth would have liked to add 'and I don't care'.)

Have you ever considered how often we tell lies to children? We might be surprised to find out just how often we use techniques like this:

> 'I don't know the answer. You'll have to tell me.'

It could be worth noting how such 'lies' are perceived, and responded to, by individuals or groups in the class.

Joking in the classroom

Joking can serve a number of functions in the classroom. If we seek to embarrass a child, to make him or her 'feel a fool', joking is being used as a means of social control. However, joking may also serve as a way out of embarrassing situations or confrontations. Often joking is used as a means of contact or as an entry point into a relationship. It is also used to individualise and make more intimate an ongoing relationship. It can be used simply to present an atmosphere of fun and conviviality.

The sort of joking that occurs most commonly in school is not much concerned with punch-line gags. It involves relationships suffused with a humour that often depends upon a shared background of experience. Often the 'joke' is revealed through underplayed status or mock authority. To an observer, joking in the classroom often seems like over-familiarity, but it is one way in which social structures can be made 'human'. Through joking the participants are allowed to reveal their *personal* identities, despite the *social* identities conferred upon them by their status.

Through this sort of joking we become both more accessible and more vulnerable, because we break the usual conventions associated with our teacher status. At the same time joking gives us access to the child in a way which is not possible within the constraints of our social identity. Thus it raises the question of defining where person/person relationships end and teacher/pupil relationships are re-established. If we joke with (not at) our pupils, we must be prepared for the unexpected. We must be prepared to become the butt of the joke. We must be prepared to allow pupils access to power because joking marks and creates areas of negotiation, areas where relationships are flexible and open to change.

The following exchange clearly illustrates these shifts in power. (Note also the teacher 'lie' that occurs halfway through.)

MR A: Next one. What do they call a man who does magic in Africa?

CHILDREN: Sir! Sir! Witch doctor.

MR A: Which doctor? I don't know.

CHILDREN: *(laughing)* A *witch* doctor! No, a *witch* doctor!

MR A: Yes, sometimes called Dr Who.
(Laughter)

MR A: Yes — a *witch* doctor.
(Amused talk)

MR A: I spent — I stayed up all last night learning all these jokes so I'd be ready for you this morning.
(Jennifer makes a remark inaudible to the rest of the class)

MR A: Did you hear that?

CHILDREN: No! *(Laughter)* What?
(Silence)

MR A: You know we were talking about revolutionaries yesterday!

CHILDREN: *(nodding agreement)* Yeah!

MR A: Here! — Class 15's own revolutionary. When I said I'd stayed up all night learning my jokes, she turned round to me — complete straight face — and said, 'What a waste of time!' *(Laughter)*

We might find it useful to monitor our joking behaviour. Do we joke with or at particular children? Does the recognised class jester act as a spokesman, testing limits for the class, or is he or she 'used' by us to demonstrate such limits? Are 'harmless' jokes actually perceived as hurtful by the child at whom they are directed (and why were they made in the first place)? Do all children share in the joke or are some children left out — the joke being 'on' them rather than 'with' them? How do we react when we become the butt of the joke? Where do we draw our boundaries in terms of who may be involved, when joking may be allowed and on what topics, and where it may occur?

Transmitting attitudes and expectations through talk

We are all aware that we make changes to our speech according to the topic, the situation, and the audience. The way we ask the boss for a raise is different from the way we ask a mate for a cigarette. However, we are less aware of the motivations and social consequences which underlie changes in our speech styles.

It would seem that if we wish to indicate that we like someone, we make an attempt to become more like them (*to converge*) both in *what* we say and in *how* we say it. We avoid jargon or technical language if we believe this will create difficulties for our listener. We tend to use the sort of language he or she would use. We may even make a shift in accent. On the other hand we often move away (*diverge*) from those we don't like. We make no attempt to simplify or elaborate our ideas or to use language with which our listener will be comfortable.

Thus there's an obvious value for teachers in monitoring the converging and diverging moves they make in their interactions with children. But the question for teachers is not merely, 'Did I converge or diverge?' The important questions are: 'Why did I shift? How? To what extent?' and, perhaps most importantly, 'With what effect?'

If we tape some of our interactions with our class and ask ourselves these questions as we listen to our tapes, we may become more sensitive to the intended and unintended consequences of our interactions with individuals, small groups or the whole class.

In a nutshell, then, the theory holds that against the background of our experience, beliefs and intentions we attribute certain motives, intentions and abilities to our pupils, thus converging on or diverging from their language behaviour and signalling through our language, gestures, tone of voice, body movements and so on our own values and attitudes towards them.

This is not to say that convergence is necessarily 'a good thing' and divergence necessarily 'a bad thing'. If we as teachers indicate a more appropriate pronunciation of a word used by a pupil; if we deliberately introduce technical or more complex items, or if we indicate disagreement with aspects of a child's performance, we may do so in an attempt to foster the child's development. However, for such a strategy to be successful, divergence at one level may need to be balanced by convergence at others. This may be perceived in the following interaction, where the teacher of a class of 11-12-year-olds is talking to Mark about his attempt at creating a cartoon strip. He begins by reading the caption:

> '"*I'm the ghost of the white eyes.*"
> '"*If you don't shut up you'll be the ghost of the black eyes.*"

'Aah! That's all I need!' He chuckles.

'OK. That's not bad at all. Now the thing is — ah — you've got to change those around haven't you — in each case, see? P'raps it might be an idea to move the — have the reception table there — of the hotel — and — ah Mr Invisible coming in. Who's this — Mr Square? — coming in?

'I like this idea where you put — put the time of day in — time of night, I should say.

'Now, that's not a very good picture though, is it? — that one th‿.e — nor's that.

'I like the idea though.

'Now we need to polish up on the pictures — right? — and get the words in the right order.'

Here the divergence is at the level of content, yet even at this level it is interesting to note how the teacher alternates converging and diverging shifts.

'OK. That's not bad at all…. the thing is you've got to change those around….'

'I like this idea…. Now, that's not a very good picture though, is it?…'

'I like the idea though…. Now we need to polish up….'

What the transcript can't show (but the tape clearly does) is that although the teacher is diverging at the content level, his tone of voice, his pace, and his laughter are all supportive. (His chuckles indicate that the apparently divergent 'That's all I need!' is really a convergent move.)

As teachers, then, we may converge or diverge for a variety of motives and on a variety of linguistic levels. It also seems that some combination of speech shifts may be perceived by a listener as *optimally* convergent, whereas maximal convergence may be perceived as patronising, ingratiating, or even threatening (see Giles 1978).

To see how an awareness of this may influence a speaker, let's look at the patterns of convergence and divergence in another transcript, taken from a different segment of the same cartoon-strip lesson.

1	T:	Ohhh!! Terrible joke! Terrible story!
2	PAUL:	I never thought it was a terrible story.
3	T:	Actually — it's not really. It's just that it's so silly.
4	PAUL:	I made it up.
5	T:	Yeah! I know *(laughing)*. It looks like it Paul. No actually — I'm being — I'm being rather mean. It's not all that bad — it's just that — um — no — in fact, actually it's quite good I suppose — the twin brother —
6		You can use that idea of somebody speaking out of a picture

		once — p'raps twice — but I think using it three times is — yeah? — a little bit — bit too —
7		Now, let me see — oh, this is with that — oh, I see, it's — um — it's Bubble's twin brother that sticks one on.
8	PAUL:	No sir — ah — sir — ah! This is — sir — he thinks it's — um — him, but it's his twin brother.
9	T:	That's right.
10	PAUL:	He gets 'em all into trouble — so he hits him.
11	T:	Right. Um — yeah! To — wh — can you give your — your bubbles — make them, make them a little bit bigger — all right? Like this — they're a little bit too small.
12		OK — um — now that's one, two, three, four, five, six, seven, eight, nine, ten — right! There's twelve frames there, all right?
13		Um — that should make an excellent cartoon when you've finished.
14		Um — I think actually — just for the effort that you put into the — this part — I'll give you two stars for that —
15		because you've obviously — uh — taken a lot of time and trouble over it —
16		and — uh — just because you happen to have an appreciative teacher.

In the opening exchange Paul's teacher inadvertently goes beyond the optimal level of divergence and is misunderstood. Noting Paul's obvious distress, the teacher both converges and diverges in statement 3. Again he is misunderstood, and again, in 5, he converges not only in content, but in tone and pace and by laughing. In 6, he begins to diverge, senses possible further danger, and switches, in 7, from a more neutral position to the converging 'sticks one on.' By 13, he is still converging — 'terrible joke' has now become 'excellent cartoon'. In addition, in 14, the effort as well as the product is praised. However, by 15 and 16, although Paul is now happily accepting his teacher's statements, the teacher is beginning to sense that he is running the risk of going too far and feels constrained to justify the magnitude of his shift to himself as well as to Paul.

Have I challenged you to make an attempt to monitor your own language behaviour? While it is difficult to teach and listen to yourself teach at the same time, self-monitoring is possible if you leave a tape recorder running while you are talking (a video recorder would be even better) and then listen in a focussed way to the interactions that occurred. Remember the question is not merely, 'Did I converge or diverge?' You should also ask yourself, 'Why did I shift? How? To what extent?' and, perhaps most importantly, 'With what effect?'

As well as noting the effects of deliberate shifts, you may become more aware of shifts you had not planned and of their effects. You may also find it useful to relate the concept of 'optimal' levels to the reactions of particular children.

You might like to listen to, and think about, your interactions with the whole class, or you may prefer to focus more closely on your relationships with an individual or a small group. Similarly, you might like to consider all the sections of questions listed below or you may prefer to concentrate on only one or some of them.

Listen and ask yourself...

Lesson goals

- Did I perceive emerging opportunities or did I miss them because I was pursuing 'my' objectives?

- Did my response/lack of response/minimal response to what could have been a promising initiative from a child have subsequent effects on that child (or on the discussion itself)?

- Did children understand my terms/language? Did I attempt to meet their needs?

Teaching role

- Did I value children's contributions? Did I display interest in the content of children's talk or did I respond within a corrective frame of reference? Whose opinions were finally accepted?

- How did I initiate and close interactions? Did I offend any child? How? Why?

Organising talk

- Who controlled (and how) the channels of communication? The amount of talk? The content of talk?

- Who did most of the talking? Why? Did opportunities for children to talk emerge naturally or did they have to be 'told' to talk?

- Was children's talk interrupted? By whom? With what effect?

- What were the effects of the above on groups/individuals?

Orders and instructions

- Did I establish 'contexts' for orders and instructions to be carried out? Did I define clearly to whom the orders and instructions applied?

- Would any child have perceived me as unfair? As 'picking on' him or her?

Questions

- Who initiated questions (and topics)? Were they open or closed?

- Were children's responses valued? Did I repeat their answers? Why? With what effect?

- What are the implications of unexpected answers (including answers not 'heard' at the time)?

- How did I react to 'insufficient' answers?

Children's feelings and attitudes

- Would any child have felt very pleased/uncomfortable/unfairly singled out/embarrassed/hurt?

- Would an impartial observer deduce that I like/dislike particular children?

- Did I convey interest in what individuals had to say? How? (Why not?)

- Did the tone of my voice (warmth/coolness), intonation, speech rate, pause and utterance lengths, pronunciation, language form (style/complexity) convey intended/unintended messages? To whom? With what effect?

- Did I use sarcasm or disparaging remarks? With what effect? On whom?

- Did I sometimes 'tell lies'? With what effect?

- Did I use words which conveyed (value) judgements, or words to 'distance' myself? With what effect?

- To whom did I distribute approval/disapproval? What did I approve/disapprove? How did I show approval/disapproval? To what extent did the values implied 'match' children's values?

- Did jokes occur? With/at the children? Who initiated them? Why? With what effect?

- If I had the opportunity, which of my statements would I rephrase? Which of my actions would I change?

Children's language

- How often did I comment on aspects of children's language? What aspects? Why? With what effect?

- Did I use 'in-group' forms? When? Why? With what effect?

I realise that self-monitoring takes time — one of the teacher's most valuable commodities. In addition, some teachers may see self-monitoring as threatening (although you can lock yourself and the tape recorder away and 'wipe' the tape after playback). There is also a danger that too great a concern with the language of communication may, in itself, adversely affect the quality of that communication. For instance, a teacher, surprised to note how often and in what ways he or she converges on the child's language style, may try to avoid this strategy (or alternatively overdo it) without considering the reasons for, or the effectiveness of, his or her previous behaviour.

In spite of all this, I hope you're prepared to accept the challenge, to listen to yourself and to talk about your teacher talk.

Note

This chapter has drawn heavily on a series of articles I published in *The Aboriginal Child at School: A National Journal for Teachers of Aboriginals* (Vol. 7, No. 3, June 1979; Vol. 8, No. 3, June 1980; Vol. 9, No. 4, August/September 1981). A companion article was published with the title 'Jennifer' in SET, No. 1, 1982.

'They Put Kisses All Over Your Book'

John Dwyer

How do children know when the teacher is pleased with them and with the work they do? How do they know when the teacher doesn't like them? How do they know when the teacher's joking, and how can it be that some jokes are funny and some are not? What is a 'good teacher'? What is 'hard' work? Are teachers 'fair'?

I put these questions to a small group of 11-year-old boys. Their comments, as they work with each other and me to clarify their meanings, are interesting and challenging. They reveal themselves as astute observers, listeners and commentators.

The transcript illustrates how hard they work to achieve a shared meaning. Their comments are interactive, overlapping and punctuated by asides.

At a more technical level the transcript indicates how non-standard and fragmentary actual talk is. This is just as true of my language as interviewer as it is of that of the children.

The transcript highlights quite vividly some of the differences between written and spoken language. The audio tape deals with overlapping comments and adds meaning through intonation in ways which cannot be captured in writing. (A video tape would have added a range of other features — body language, eye contact and so on). Having grappled with the task, I know that it is very difficult to 'write talk' without distorting its freshness and vibrancy.

However, let's listen to the children as they speak for themselves.

How do you know when a teacher's pleased with your work?

JD: How do you know when a teacher's pleased with the work you've been doing?

MARK: They put kisses all over your book.
(Laughter)

DAVE: No! Not really kisses.

MARK: X's — kisses.
(Laughter)

MARK: That's all wrong.

DAVE: No. Well our teachers —

MARK: Laugh!

DAVE: They laugh. They put 'Good' in your book. Sometimes he even gives you stars. That's what Mr A does.

JD: Mm.

MARK: Oh — once in every bicentennial year.

DAVE: *(laughing)* No — but he's a good teacher — Mr A.

MARK: Yeah.

DAVE: We like him very much.

JD: Mm! I see. Yeah. Why do you like him? What are the good things about him?

PAUL: He larks about during lesson times. Like —

DAVE: Yeah.

MARK: Yeah.

PAUL: when he's writin' somethin' — he starts muckin' about an' everything.

DAVE: An' he really —

PAUL: *(interrupting)* He starts muckin' —

DAVE: An' he really makes us laugh.

MARK: He walks by an' he always tell you that his hand slips an' he bumps you round the earhole.

DAVE: Yeah. I know — he really makes you laugh, our teacher.

PAUL: When — when he's telling a story and Jennifer F, or when she's doing maths —

DAVE: Oh yeah!

PAUL: an' Jennifer F goes, '*That's* not right!' —

DAVE: *(interrupting)* An' he goes —

PAUL: Mr A goes *(makes exclamatory gesture)* — an' carries on talkin' —

JD: With his hands. Yes, mm.

DAVE: Or either he goes, 'Tch! Another one of her sleepy jokes comin' out.'

As the boys discuss this question, laughing at the recollection of their teachers' approval, it is interesting to note how quickly they move away from teacher actions (putting crosses or 'good' in your book, giving stars) to teacher talk. These boys know their teacher is pleased with their work when he is pleased with *them*.

How do you know when teachers are pleased with YOU?

JD: How do you know when teachers are pleased with you —
           not so much with writing work — but say when you've been
           discussing or talking — how do you know they're pleased
           with you then?

DAVE: They say it.

MARK: They make jokes with you.

DAVE: Yeah, an' they tell you it was good.

JD: Mm.

DAVE: An' sometimes they even — oh sometimes they pat you —

JD: Yeah.

DAVE: *(musingly)* — tell you it's good.

PAUL: Say sometimes...they say 'That's good.'

DAVE: Yeah.

MARK: Yeah.

PAUL: They say 'You know a lot.'

JD: Do you ever know — even if they don't say anything — how
           can you tell then?

DAVE: By the expression on their face.

MARK: Mm.

PAUL: Mm.

MARK: They laugh.

DAVE: Yeah.

PAUL: Yeah.

MARK: Yeah. I can always tell when Mr J's pleased.

JD: Mm. *(Laughter)*

MARK: He give you a smackin' great big pat on the back — yowtch!

Teachers *tell* you when they're pleased with you, sometimes directly, sometimes through jokes, sometimes through facial expressions or other body
language. Even pats, 'smackin' great big pats', convey teacher pleasure
when they are part of a joke.

Are teachers' jokes always funny?

JD: When teachers joke with you and lark around, are they
           always pleased with you — or are they sometimes angry with
           you when they do that?

DAVE: No sir. They're always pleased.

PAUL: They're always pleased 'cause Mr A, when somebody's done
           good work — like John H or anything like that —

DAVE: *(interrupting)* he starts makin' some jokes about them —

PAUL: *(ignoring interruption)* he — like makes jokes against — about
           the person.

DAVE: *(continuing unchecked)* when he's in a bad mood.

JD: But then do you know then that he's not pleased — when he makes those jokes?

DAVE: Yes sir.

PAUL: Yes sir.

JD: Well how do you know the difference? You know sometimes....

PAUL: Sir — some jokes are funny and some jokes ain't.

JD: How do you mean?

MARK: Like he tells the jokes an' then he does — he looks serious.

DAVE: Yeah! — and the expression on his face — he looks really mad. Sometimes — once John H, he kept answering sir back and sir said that was enough — an' he kept doin' it, didn't he? —

MARK: Yeah.

PAUL: Yeah.

DAVE: An' he really got sir mad — he was in a bad mood all day then.

JD: Mm. And was he mad with the rest of you then?

BOYS: No. Not the rest of us — just John H.

DAVE: We cooled him down though afterwards, didn't we?

MARK: Just!

DAVE: Yeah. Just!

JD: I'm interested in that about jokes though — that difference — you can tell sometimes when it's a funny joke —

BOYS: Yeah.

JD: and sometimes when it's a serious joke. How do you tell — just by the look on his face?

BOYS: Yeah.

JD: Does he say the same things or does he say different things?

PAUL: When he says the joke starting — he means to make funny — like — he laughs after the joke — y'know he's joking.

DAVE: Or the other one —

MARK: *(interrupting)* Or sometimes when he's got a good joke he makes — he tells the joke and then he goes — then he goes *(grimaces)* he looks at you —

DAVE: *(nodding)* Yeah. I know.

MARK: an' you know he ain't serious.

JD: I see. So it's not just the joke — it's the joke and the face he pulls —

BOYS: Yeah.

JD: or something like that, so if it's a serious joke it's a different sort of face.

BOYS: Yeah.

JD: Huh huh — oh that's good.

These boys have no difficulty in agreeing that some jokes are funny and some are not. Teacher's jokes are funny and meant to be fun when the teacher jokes *with* you. But, as Paul hints, they cease to be funny when the teacher jokes *about* you.

What is the difference between hard work and easy work?

JD: Um — have you ever had a teacher that you thought didn't like you?

DAVE: I have.

MARK: I have.

JD: How did you know or what made you think that the teacher didn't like you?

DAVE: Well he was always mad.

MARK: He set you hard work.

DAVE: Yeah I know — he set you hard work. You go to do something like talk — he was on top of you like a ton of bricks. *(Laughter)*

JD: Does a teacher who — who likes you — do they set hard work too?

DAVE: No sir.

PAUL: Well sort of —

DAVE: They set — set the same work — if they're in a good mood — but it's not all that hard — if you lie your mind to it right — you can do it.

MARK: Say it's a project — you want to do project all day — just set your mind to doing project and you can do it you know —

DAVE: and cut out everything else.

MARK: 'Cause sir helps you, he tells you jokes about it, he talks, lectures an' anything like that.

JD: So — are you doing hard work for a good teacher — who likes you?

BOYS: No sir.

DAVE: It's not hard work.

MARK: It would be hard work — if he didn't tell us how to do it.

DAVE: Yeah.

JD: Oh I see. So he helps you with it — so that — yeah!

DAVE: Yeah, but he's really mad when he explains something — um — and some people don't understand, and they don't even put their hand up and tell him.

JD: Right. Now what about the teacher that didn't like you? You said he used to give you hard work. What did you mean by that then?

DAVE: Yeah — if he gives you hard — he give you hard work and if you didn't understand something, you'd have to work it out yourself and not go up to him — he won't do nothing.

JD: Oh, I see — right!

JD: *(to Mark)* And did you say you ever had a teacher that didn't like you?

MARK: Yeah.

JD: How did you know about that teacher?

MARK: She used to shout at me a lot.

JD: Yeah.

DAVE: My teacher used to keep pickin' on me.

BOYS: Yeah.

JD: What about you Paul? Have you had — or have you been lucky — all your teachers have liked you?

PAUL: One hasn't.

JD: Well, how did you know? What happened?

PAUL: She always used to push me around — at school.

JD: Why did she do that?

PAUL: I don't know — she's got — sometimes she — er — you can't understand something — you go up to her and tell her — *(assuming teacher voice)* 'Yeah. Well I *told* you on the blackboard' — 'n all that stuff.

JD: So she'd get angry because you couldn't do your work. Did she ever get angry because you used to play up? — Did you play up?

PAUL: I don't — can't remember anything.

JD: No — when — the teachers who used to pick on you that you didn't like — I mean that didn't like you — used you work all right for them? — or was it some of your fault too?

DAVE: It was some of our fault...my fault.

MARK: Yeah. If she — if my teacher picked on me you know, I just looked at her in a funny way and for the rest of the day she wouldn't talk to me....

JD: Mm.

MARK: She just put the work down.

JD: Which used to happen first? She made you angry or you made her angry?

DAVE: She made us angry.

It would seem that whether work is 'hard' or 'easy' has very little to do with the work itself. What is important is whether the teacher helps you or not. When the teacher likes you, the work is not hard 'if you lie your mind to it', because the teacher 'helps you, he tells you jokes about it, he talks, lectures an' anything like that.'

If the teacher doesn't like you, the work is hard because 'you'd have to work it out yourself and not go up to him — he won't do nothing.' Indeed, the response is likely to be, 'Yeah. Well I *told* you on the blackboard' and 'all that stuff.'

So teachers who don't like you don't help you and get angry if you seek help. Of course, as Dave tells us, teachers who do like you and do help you also get angry, but only if you *don't* seek help.

Are teachers always fair?

JD: Yeah. OK. Um — do you think that teachers are always fair?

PAUL: Oh yeah.

DAVE: Yeah. Some of them.

MARK: Some of them.

DAVE: Not all of them.

PAUL: In this school everyone's fair.

JD: That's good. Yeah — well what about teachers who aren't fair? Do you ever see any of those sort of teachers — or do you know about those sort of teachers who aren't fair?

DAVE: Not that I know of.

PAUL: Me too.

MARK: *(smiling)* I only know one teacher.

DAVE: Which one?

MARK: Mr J...*(laughter)* and Mr B.

JD: I don't know the names anyway so you needn't say the names — but — what do you mean when they're not fair? What sort of things happen?

MARK: In rounders — he says he's —

DAVE: *(talking over Mark)* He goes like that and misses it.

MARK: *(ignoring interruption)* he's going to bowl the ball —

JD: Mm.

MARK: Well you know — you're not supposed to leave your post till he — lets go the ball — an' Mr B goes —

DAVE: *(interrupting)* He pretends to do it.

MARK: *(ignoring interruption)* he — he throws it in the air 'n he catches it again.

JD: Oh but that's probably only fooling with you, is he?

DAVE: Yeah.

MARK: *(ignoring JD's comment)* He throws it an' catches it —

DAVE: Yes, but that —

MARK: *(ignoring interruption)* an' then you're out because you've already run.

JD: Oh well, he's probably trying to teach you something too.

DAVE: That's when he's in a bad mood, he does that.

JD: But he's probably trying to teach you a rule. But I was thinking more about — you know — where you think that a teacher — uh — maybe — is not fair to you and is fair to the other kids or something like that. Can you think of anything like that?

PAUL: John H. Sometimes....

MARK: He brings it on himself. It's his fault.

DAVE: Who? John H?

MARK: Yeah.

JD: Why does he bring it on himself?

MARK: Well he's always cheeky to the teachers. 'Cause this morning he had a fight with his mum.

JD: Yeah. Mm. That sometimes happens I guess.

DAVE: I had a fight this morning.

JD: Did you? What, with your mum?

DAVE: No *(laughs)*.

MARK: No — with Darryl H. He'll kill him — put him into hospital.

JD: Gee. Do you get into trouble when you do that?

DAVE: Sometimes. I never got into trouble just now.

JD: Good.

DAVE: Maybe I'll get into trouble a bit later on.

It is reassuring to find that these boys readily agree that most teachers are fair. Even when they pick on boys like John H, they're fair because 'he brings it on himself.'

The only time a teacher's fairness is doubted is when his action makes a fool of someone. This reminds me of the jokes issue. A joke is funny so long as a teacher jokes *with* you and not *at* you. A teacher is fair so long as he doesn't trick you or belittle you.

A group of 11-year-old girls with whom I discussed these same issues gave responses which were markedly similar, and it is worth noting how often both groups referred to teacher talk and other linguistic features. Perhaps Jennifer deserves the last word:

JENNIFER: When we have — when Mr A — um — he goes, 'Now hearken to my words of wisdom' — and we all start laughing.

JD: Why do you laugh at that?

JENNIFER: Um — because — um —

CAROLINE: We all tell him he doesn't know anything.

JD: Do you laugh at the way he says that?

ALL: Yes! Yes!

JENNIFER: He says it as if he's God....

'Assessing Oral Language'

John Dwyer

So your children are talking in class — as individuals, in pairs, in small and large groups.

But is their talk productive or is it just noise? Is it possible to assess talking and listening and why should we try? What rationale would underlie any such assessment? What might be assessed and how?

In this chapter I would like to consider four issues:

Purposes — why assess oral language?

Principles — what underpins the assessment of oral language?

Priorities — what is to be assessed?

Practices — how are talking and listening to be assessed?

Purposes — why assess oral language?

There are numerous reasons for attempting the assessment of talking and listening. Some are included in the diagram opposite.

A more concise justification was offered by eleven-year-old Elizabeth. After having an exciting and challenging talking/listening assessment task outlined to her, she commented,

> 'That's a good idea. We spend most of our lives talking so we ought to know if we're good at it.'

Principles — what underpins the assessment of oral language?

If the assessment of talking and listening (and indeed of any aspect of language) is to be effective, I believe that it needs to be based on a number

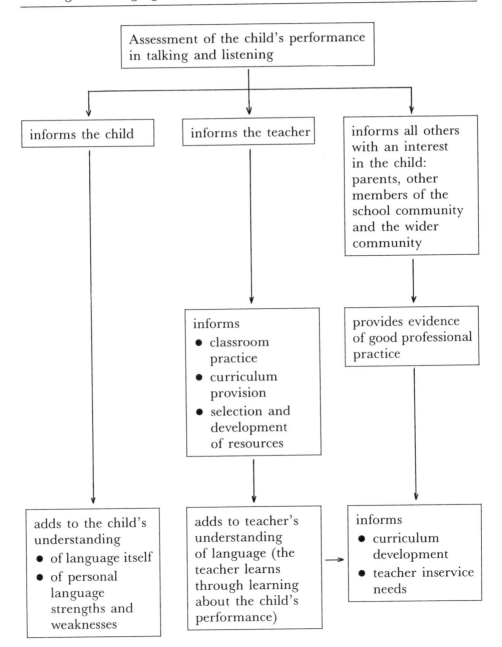

Purposes for Assessing Oral Language

of underlying principles, some of which refer to assessment itself, and some of which arise from a particular view of language. If assessment is not based on these principles, the processes used and the language products assessed will be haphazard, and the results obtained will provide only limited information for both learner and teacher.

Principles which underpin assessment in general

- Assessment must be fair to all. In particular, it must be fair to girls and to children from differing social and cultural backgrounds.

- Assessment should be an integral part of the educational process, continually providing both 'feedback' and 'feedforward'.

- Assessment should pay attention to the process as well as the product of the task.

- Assessment practices should reflect what is known about good educational practice.

- Assessment practices should provide opportunities for self-assessment and evaluation by teachers and pupils and should encourage pupils to see themselves as active participators in assessment and evaluation processes.

- Assessment policies and practices are critically dependent on the quality of interpretation of the results obtained.

Principles which underpin the assessment of talking and listening in particular

This book has presented a view of language as a collaborative, meaning-making process whereby it is shaped according to the contexts in which it is used and the purposes for which it is used.

Such a view of language generates a number of principles which should underpin the assessment of talking and listening.

- Talk is purposeful. Through it we do things and get things done in collaboration with others. Assessment of talking and listening should reflect this.

- A successful communicator needs to master a range of competencies. Assessment should sample the variety and complexity of spoken language.

- Oral language is important in all areas of the primary school curriculum. Talk assists learning in all school subjects. Assessment of oral language should make use of cross-curriculum opportunities.

- Talking and writing are integral parts of a child's overall communicative ability. Children often have to read about a topic, talk about it with others, and write a report that draws on both the reading and the discussion. Some assessment procedures should be multi-modal and should involve sequential activities.

- Talking and listening occur together. Assessment procedures should not separate them artificially.

- Spoken language is sensitive to context. Speakers are always influenced by such contextual factors as the subject matter, the social roles and relationships of the people involved in the interaction, the degree of formality that exists, and the nature and interpretation of the 'feedback' given and received. Assessment of oral communication must recognise and take account of these factors.

- Attitudes and oral language performance are interrelated. Some attention should be given to the assessment of pupils' attitudes towards talking and listening in various school and school-related settings.

(adapted from Maclure and Hargreaves 1986, p. 2)

Perhaps all of the above can be summed up if we ask ourselves a few simple but significant questions.

- Does this kind of assessment mesh with my beliefs about learning, teaching and language?

- Does it allow me to become aware of, and meet, the needs of the child (the learner), and does it allow the child to become more aware of his or her own strengths and needs?

- Does it allow me to focus on future learning? (Could I claim that I assess, not to prove but to improve?)

Priorities — what is to be assessed?

Children use spoken language constantly in school. Not all of this language can be assessed, nor should it be. The challenge is to conceive of, foster and assess language development in terms which are broad enough to accommodate the wide variations among individuals in the learning sequences they follow, and in the cumulative process through which they acquire an increasing grasp of language and increasing sophistication in its use.

One way of meeting this challenge is to develop a theoretical framework against which you can prepare assessment tasks and procedures which suit the detailed program in operation in your class.

The *P-10 Language Education Framework*, recently released by the Queensland Education Department, suggests that teachers can assess children's language at a *holistic* level, in terms of language in use, and at an *analytic* level, in terms of attitudes, processes, skills and knowledge. Using the details provided in that document (p. 43) it is possible to develop an oral language assessment framework, as shown in the table below.

Holistic assessment of child's oral language	Oral language in use	Does the child: • use a variety of kinds of talk (genres)? • suit talk to the social setting?
Analytic assessment of child's oral language	Attitudes	Does the child: • express self-confidence as a talker? • enjoy using language? • respect the culture and language of others?
	Processes	Does the child: • use talking and listening to organise experiences, information, ideas and opinions? • use talk to confirm, predict, reflect, infer, analyse, synthesise, hypothesise, evaluate?
	Skills	Does the child: • use appropriate generic structure, vocabulary, grammar, intonation, pronunciation, and non-verbal communication? • talk cohesively? • attend to the needs of his/her audience?
	Knowledge of attitudes, processes and skills	Does the child have explicit knowledge about: • his/her own language attitudes, thinking processes, communication procedures, special uses of language? • aspects of the social context? • aspects of language features?

An Oral Language Assessment Framework

A second approach to this challenge is to try to define a series of attainment targets in language. Once again the task is to define targets broad enough to accommodate the wide diversity of performance among individuals, and yet not so broad as to be virtually meaningless and non-assessable.

In England this task has been attempted by the National Curriculum Committee for *English for Ages 5-11*, which reported in November 1988. That committee was guided by the report of the earlier *Task Group on Assessment and Testing* (January 1988), which had suggested the development of school subjects described in terms of profile components. Each component would have a defined attainment target to be achieved at a number of specified levels. (For core subjects, such as English, which extend across the age range 5 to 16 years, there were to be ten levels.) Importantly, the levels were not to be related to pupil ages or years of schooling. It was expected that for any given age group pupil performance would fall across a range of levels, with the range widening as pupils became older.

Against this background the *English for Ages 5-11* report proposed this attainment target for speaking and listening (one of the profile components of English):

> *Pupils should demonstrate their understanding of the spoken word and the capacity to express themselves effectively in a variety of speaking and listening activities, matching style and response to audience and purpose.*
>
> Paragraph 8.12

This broad attainment target was then broken down to five levels of attainment in speaking and listening across the ages 5 to 11. They are shown in the table overleaf (based on Paragraph 8.15).

While it is important to remember that these attainment targets apply specifically to the National Curriculum proposed for England and Wales, they may help you to establish talking and listening benchmarks related to the curriculum in operation in your school. Remember that such attainment targets can be applied to talking and listening activities across the total curriculum.

A third way of meeting this challenge was developed by the Assessment of Performance Unit (APU — a unit within the Department of Education and Science for England and Wales) when it first undertook the assessment of speaking and listening in 1982 and 1983.

The. APU decided to focus on the purposes for which oral language is used — purposes such as describing, specifying, informing, expounding, instructing, directing, reporting, narrating, arguing, persuading, questioning, discussing, evaluating evidence, speculating and advancing hypotheses.

The assessment tasks designed by the APU asked pupils to carry out activities involving talking and listening which were similar to those they

Level	Pupils should be able to...
1	Speak freely, and listen, one-to-one to a peer group member. Respond to simple classroom instructions given by a teacher.
2	In a range of activities (including problem-solving) speak freely, and listen, to a small group of peers.
	Listen attentively, and respond, to stories and poetry.
	Speak freely to the teacher, listen and make verbal and non-verbal responses as appropriate.
	Respond to an increasing range and complexity of classroom instructions.
3	Present real or imaginary events in a connected narrative to a small group of peers, speaking freely and audibly.
	Convey accurately a simple message.
	Give and receive simple instructions and respond appropriately.
	Listen attentively for increased periods of time and respond as appropriate.
4	Describe an event or experience to a group of peers, clearly, audibly and in detail.
	Give and receive precise instructions and follow them.
	Ask relevant questions with increasing confidence.
	Offer a reasoned explanation of how a task has been done or a problem has been solved.
	Take part effectively in a small group discussion and respond to others in the group.
	Make confident use of the telephone.
	Speak freely and audibly to a class.
	Speak freely and audibly to the adults encountered in school.
5	Speak freely and audibly to a larger audience of peers and adults.
	Discuss and debate constructively, advocating and justifying a particular point of view.
	Contribute effectively to a small group discussion which aims to reach agreement on a given assignment.

Attainment Targets: Speaking and Listening (Ages 5-11)

might encounter in school or everyday life. In selecting and developing the tasks the following issues were kept in mind:

- For what purposes do pupils tend to use sustained talk in the classroom and outside it?

- To whom do they address such talk?

- For what purposes and in what context do they listen to and interpret such talk?

The assessment activities developed involved such tasks as:

- describing pictures to a listener who then had to identify them
- interpreting an account of a process (assisted by diagrams)
- constructing a model, following a sequence of oral instructions given by a friend
- interpreting a story and then retelling it to others
- speculating on the reasons for an experimental finding.

The majority of the tasks had different components involving both the interpretation and the production of sustained talk. Speaking and listening were not separated artificially.

Some tasks involved a sequence of language activities. For example, one pupil might be asked to interpret an account of a science experiment and then instruct another pupil in how to carry it out. The second pupil would then describe the results of the experiment and both might report on what was perceived.

Some talking and listening tasks also incorporated other language modes such as reading and writing as a prelude to talk or as an outcome of it. A number of activities focussed on subject areas other than English (see Gorman et al. 1988, p. 5).

These functional tasks may suggest a model which you can apply to the work of your class.

I started this section with a question,

> What talking and listening should be assessed?

and a challenge,

> We need to ensure that any assessment takes account of the complexity of oral language in use and also allows for the wide variation of performance within and among individuals.

I have suggested three possible responses to this challenge:

- the development of an oral language framework against which assessment tasks and procedures can be prepared

- the defining of a series of attainment targets against which the performance of individual children can be measured

- a functional tasks approach.

It is now *your* challenge. I want to move on to a new one.

Practices — how are talking and listening to be assessed?

At the outset we need to remember that assessment is not synonymous with testing. Oral language can be assessed in a variety of ways which may or may not include direct testing.

Ideally, assessment of oral language involves children and teachers in observing, monitoring and analysing children's oral language performance during normal school and classroom activities. Assessment may focus on language processes or on language products.

Evidence can be gathered through conferences, interviews, discussions, direct questioning and listening. These techniques can be supplemented by using audiotapes and videotapes, checklists, anecdotal records, questionnaires, and inventories.

Children can also help to monitor oral language itself and how it supports teaching and learning. For example, a questionnaire could include such items as:

- How much time do *you* think should be spent in school on *learning how to...*

	A LOT	SOME	NOT MUCH
give a clear, spoken description of events?	☐	☐	☐
share information by talking about it?	☐	☐	☐
talk about personal thoughts and feelings?	☐	☐	☐

- How true is each statement for *you*?

'I *learn* best when...

	YES	NOT SURE	NO
I work with friends on our own project.'	☐	☐	☐
the teacher reads some information and we talk about it.'	☐	☐	☐

- Do you think children should speak differently in the classroom from the way they speak in the playground? Explain your answer.

There may be times, of course, when you want to use a test to assess some aspects of a child's oral language performance. Such tests are often teacher-prepared, in which case they are usually closely related to the classroom program and to the teaching and learning that the child has experienced.

Occasionally you may wish to use standardised test materials. Because these involve assessment based on standardised content and standardised administrative procedures and methods of scoring, they need to be used with discrimination and the results obtained need to be interpreted with care and sensitivity. This is particularly true when the tests are used with children from differing cultural and linguistic backgrounds.

The APU has been developing and using some exciting materials and procedures for testing speaking and listening. Many teachers have used these materials and procedures as models for developing similar tests more closely related to the actual language program operating in their school.

The APU tasks are designed:

- to be as 'realistic' as possible, so that children will use the kind of language which would be expected in a non-test situation
- to put children at ease so that they will talk spontaneously and unselfconsciously
- to be stimulating and fun to take part in.

Children participate in friendship pairs or in small groups created by combining pairs. This creates a relaxed and informal setting. It also provides a genuine audience, overcoming the problem often faced by children of having to ask questions of, or explain information to, an assessor (teacher) who is obviously already 'in the know'.

Some examples (drawn from Maclure and Hargreaves 1986, pp. 15-29) may clarify the procedure.

Task 1 — An anecdote

In this task each pair of children listens to a tape recording of someone telling an anecdote as a stimulus for their own anecdotes and as a reminder of the form that anecdotes usually take. Each child is then invited to recount an anecdote of his or her own.

The purpose of this task is to elicit talk which tends towards the 'informal', which allows children to speak from their own experience, and which requires them to depict events in the past, conveying a perspective or point of view and establishing them as 'interesting' for listeners.

Task 2 — Giving an account of a process: how the garden spider builds its web

In this task one child listens to a tape recording of how the garden spider builds its web, and arranges six diagrams (supplied) to correspond with the stages in the process described on the tape. This child then recounts the stages in the process to another child who hasn't heard the tape, using the diagrams as an aid in the re-telling.

This task is designed to elicit a type of communication which involves listening to and assimilating information about a process, and then conveying this information clearly to other listeners.

Task 3 — Science experiment: giving instructions

This task is related to carrying out a simple science experiment. The first child of a pair is told that he/she will be asked to give instructions to the second, who will then carry out the experiment. The assessor shows the first child the equipment to be used and explains the instructions which are to be given to the partner. The second child returns to the room at this stage and the instructional task begins.

The purpose of this task is to elicit a type of communication which requires children to listen carefully, to give clear and explicit instructions, to transmit newly acquired information, and to use the language of science for scientific purposes.

Audio tape recordings of the performance are made by the assessor for subsequent marking and analysis. The assessor's role is to establish the context for talk and to record the talk, but not to control or direct it.

The marking procedure used for all tasks is interesting. The assessor makes various on-the-spot assessments. The tape is then assessed holistically and analytically by a number of other markers. A detailed overview of the marking procedure (adapted from Gorman 1986, p. 30) is given in the table opposite.

While this procedure is probably too complex and time-consuming for the busy classroom teacher, it does provide a model which can be adapted for classroom use. For example, the teacher could attempt some on-the-spot assessment and then check that later by assessing a taped performance. Or the teacher could assess the taped performance holistically or analytically and then check that assessment against one made independently by a colleague.

If it does nothing else the model provides an assessment framework, identifying features which can be used to assess talking and listening. (It is interesting to note its similarities to the framework set out on p. 98.)

Some teachers who have introduced modified versions of the APU tasks and procedures have found that there is value in using children as observers and assessors. From a group of four, one pair carries out the task while

> **STAGE 1   On-the-spot Assessment**
> - Overall impression of communicative effectiveness (Scale 1-7)
>
> - Orientation to listener (Scale 1-5)
>   non-verbal: eye contact, posture, gesture
>   verbal: pausing, tempo, audibility
>
> - Task-specific features (checklist)
>
> **STAGE 2   Holistic Scoring**
> - Overall impression marking (Scale 1-7)
>   (Two independent markers using tape made at time of performance)
>
> **STAGE 3   Analytic Scoring**
> - Focussed assessment of task-related criteria
>   (a) Propositional/semantic content (Scale 1-5)
>   (b) Sequential structure (Scale 1-5)
>   (c) Lexico-grammatical features (syntax, lexis) (Scale 1-5)
>   (d) Performance features (self-correction, hesitation, tempo, etc.)
>   (Scale 1-3)
>   (Two independent markers using random sub-samples of taped performances)

Assessment of APU Speaking and Listening Tasks

the other two act as observers, introducing the task, working the tape recorder, and making an on-the-spot appraisal of communicative effectiveness. Later, while listening to the tape with the teacher, they become markers. Once the categories have been explained, even quite young children can be very perceptive in assessing their own performance and that of others.

Throughout this book talking has been shown to be purposeful, varied, integrated with other modes of communication, and responsive to the contexts of its use.

It is important that its assessment is also all of these things, tapping the widest practicable range of activities and settings.

An active, creative process should be assessed in ways and by means which are themselves active and creative.

References

Bolton, R. 1987, *People Skills*, Simon & Schuster, Sydney.

Boys, J., Carr, J., Commins L., Kindt, I., Patton, W., Ralston, F. & Sachs, J 1983, *Study Talk: A Sourcebook of Language Activities*, Curriculum Development Centre, Canberra.

Britton, J. 1983, 'Writing and the story world', in *Explorations in the Development of Writing*, ed. B. Kroll & G. Wells, John Wiley, New York.

Cambourne, B. 1984, 'Language, learning and literacy', in A. Butler & J. Turbill, *Towards a Reading-Writing Classroom*, PETA, Sydney.

Cambourne, B. & Turbill, J. 1987, *Coping with Chaos*, PETA, Sydney.

Carr, J. 1984, *Talking about Talk: A Report on a Survey of Opinion*, Curriculum Services Branch, Queensland Department of Education, Brisbane.

Delamont, S. 1976, *Interaction in the Classroom*, Methuen, London.

Department of Education and Science 1988a, *National Curriculum: English for Ages 5-11*, DES & the Welsh Office, London.

Department of Education and Science 1988b, *Report of the Task Group on Assessment and Testing*, HMSO, London.

Edwards, H. 1980, *There's a Hippopotamus on Our Roof Eating Cake*, Hodder & Stoughton, London.

English for Ages 5-11; see Department of Education and Science 1988a.

Elley, W. 1982, 'Bridging the gap between 1st and 2nd language learning', in *Aboriginal Literacy: Bridging the Gap*, ed. R. Lipscombe & D. Burnes, Australian Reading Association, Adelaide.

Far Northern Schools Development Unit 1987, *Year Three Units*, FNSDU, Queensland Department of Education, Thursday Island.

Giles, H. 1978, *Sociolinguistics: A Social Psychological Approach*, Academic Press, New York.

Gordon, T. 1976, *Parent Effectiveness Training*, Effectiveness Training Inc., Melbourne.

Gorman, T. 1986, *The Framework for the Assessment of Language*, APU, NFER-Nelson, Windsor.

Gorman, T., White, J., Brooks, G., MacLure, M. & Kispal, A. 1988, *Language Performance in Schools*, APU, HMSO, London.

Gray, B. 1984, *Helping Children to Become Language Learners in the Classroom*, Northern Territory Department of Education, Darwin.

Hornsby, D., Sukarna, D. & Parry, J. 1986, *Read On: A Conference Approach to Reading*, Martin Educational, Sydney.

Johnson, T. & Louis, D. 1987, *Bringing It All Together*, Methuen, Sydney.

Kingman, J. 1988, *Report of the Committee of Inquiry into the Teaching of English Language*, HMSO, London.

Kirk, S., McCarthy, J. & Kirk, W. 1968, *Illinois Test of Psycholinguistic Abilities*, University of Illinois Press, Urbana.

Krashen, S. 1981, *Second Language Acquisition and Second Language Learning*, Pergamon Institute of English, Oxford.

Maclure, M. & Hargreaves, M. 1986, *Speaking and Listening: Assessment at Age 11*, APU, NFER-Nelson, Windsor.

Mesler, J. & Cowley, C. 1980, *Poor Old Polly*, The Story Box, Level 1, Rigby Educational Books, Brisbane.

Montgomery, B. 1982, *Coping with Stress*, Pitman Health Information Services, Melbourne.

Nash, R. 1976, 'Pupils' expectations of their teachers', in *Explorations in Classroom Observation*, ed. M. Stubbs & S. Delamont, John Wiley, New York.

Queensland Department of Education 1979, *Overview for Language Development Program: Years 1-3*, Van Leer Project, Brisbane.

Queensland Department of Education 1989, *P-10 Language Education Framework*, Brisbane.

Task Group on Assessment and Testing; see Department of Education and Science 1988b.

Wells, G. 1977, 'Language use and educational success', *Research in Education*, November 1977, pp. 9-34.